About this Guide

The aim of this guide, unique in its own  in a form easily understood by the reader date information as possible about the is combines a hotel and traveller's guide, the needs of the modern traveller.

The guide is divided into three parts. The first part gives a general account of the island and the city of Rodos, their history and a description of the main sights.

The second part has the latest list of *all* the hotels in Rodos island, listed alphabetically and within each category. Bear in mind that hotels in Rodos are rated among the most modern in the world. Most of them are newly-built and offer all the up-to-date facilities, in accordance with their classification. The information about hotels in this guide has been supplied by the hotels themselves with the vital assistance of the Hotel Owners Association of Rodos. Where information is incomplete it means that those hotels did not reply to our questionnaire or did so too late to be included in this issue. In this case the hotel category is preceded by an asterisk. At the end of this guide the reader will find an alphabetical index of all the hotels mentioned and a list of all the symbols used, along with their explanation.

Finally, there is a third part which contains a variety of practical information - from services to shopping, dining and night life-, designed to help visitors to find their way about and make the most of their stay.

A note on spelling: There hasn't yet been a generally accepted system for the transliteration of modern Greek place-names and personal names into the Latin alphabet. However, an effort has been made both by the NTOG and many scholars for the transliteration of these place-names and personal names in a form approximating to their pronunciation. Believing that this is the right thing to do, we adopted among other new forms the new transliteration of the English form "Rhodes", which is "Rodos". We have kept the form "Rhodes" in the hotel section of this guide since the hotel owners and the Hotel Owners Association of Rhodes keep to the English form of "Rhodes" than the new one "Rodos". Generally speaking we have kept the "old" forms of spelling when the texts in which they appear are not the responsibility of the editors of this guide.

3

THE ISLAND AND THE PEOPLE

Only 12 miles off the coast of Turkey, Rodos (Rhodes) is the largest of the Dodecanese islands. The name Dodecanese (" *dodeka nisi* " = twelve islands) is used to denote the complex of islands in the S.E. Aegean, also called Southern Sporades, which consists of 200 islands of all sizes and shapes, but of which only 18 are inhabited at present. Thirteen of the islands (Astypalea, Chalki, Kalimnos, Karpathos, Kassos, Kastellorizo, Kos, Leros, Nisiros , Patmos, Rodos, Simi and Tilos) have local governments,with Rodos as the administrative capital.

Rodos, the flower of the Dodecanese (" *rodon* " means "rose" in Ancient Greek), has a total area of 1,412 km (540 sq. miles) and a population of over 90,000. Almost half the population lives in the city of Rodos and the rest is dispersed among the other 44 small towns and villages throughout the island, the biggest of them being the village of Trianda, 8 km from the city of Rodos.

The island has a 220 km (138 m.) coastline full of beaches and coves. The terrain is mountainous for the most part, with a few plains, mostly near the coast. The highest mountain is Atavyros (1,215 m.), with Akramites (823 m.) and Profitis Ilias (798 m.) to follow. All the remaining mountains are much lower in height, barely justifying the name "mountain".

Cultivated farmland covers 18% of the island, the pasture land 34%, and the island forests 37%. The main agricultural products are wine, oil and tobacco. Cattle is raised throughout the island. Forest exploitation is also a source of income for the island inhabitants.

Climate

Rodos as the rest of Greece, belongs to the Mediterranean climate zone, with a mild climate. With 262 sunny days per year it is one of the sunniest islands of the Mediterranean Sea.

January and February are the coolest months of the year, July to September the warmest.

	J	F	M	A	M	J	J	A	S	O	N	D
Air temperature												
°F	54	54	55	63	70	77	81	82	78	68	61	55
°C	12	12	13	17	21	25	27	28	25	20	16	13
Water temperature												
°F	59	57	59	63	66	72	75	77	75	73	66	61
°C	15	14	15	17	19	22	24	25	24	23	19	16
Rainy days	17	12	11	7	5	1	1	1	3	8	12	16

All figures shown are approximate monthly averages.

Religion

The established church of Greece is the Greek Orthodox Church. In the diocese of the Metropolitan of Rodos belong the islands of Tilos, Nisyros, Chalki and Simi, as well as Rodos itself. The Metropolitan of Rodos plus the other three Dodecanese Metropolitans are under the Patriarch of Constantinople.

Language

The national language is modern Greek *"Dimotiki",* as opposed to the language used now only in church, the *"Katharèvousa".* In towns and villages of tourist interest English is understood by almost everybody.

The Greek alphabet is:

Letter			Pronunciation
A	α	álfa	a, semi-long, as in "apple"
B	β	víta	v
Γ	γ	gháma	gh; y before e or i
Δ	δ	dhélta	dh as in "the"
E	ε	épsilon	e, open, semi-long, as in "egg"
Z	ζ	zíta	z
H	η	íta	ee, semi-long, as in "cheese"
Θ	θ	thíta	th as in "thin"
I	ι	ióta	i, semi-long, as in "cheese"
K	κ	kápa	k, ky
Λ	λ	lámdha	l
M	μ	mi	m
N	ν	ni	n
Ξ	ξ	ksi	ks
O	o	ómikron	o, open, semi-long
Π	π	pi	p
P	ρ	ro	r, lightly rolled
Σ	σ^1	síghma	s
T	τ	taf	t
Y	υ	ípsilon	i, as in "cheese"
Φ	φ	fi	f
X	χ	khi ·	ch as in Scottish "loch"
Ψ	ψ	psi	ps
Ω	ω	omégha	o, open, semi-long

¹ written ς at the end of a word

Government

Administratively Rodos is the seat of government of the *Nomarchia* (prefecture) of the Dodecanese. Rodos has its own *dimarchos* (mayor), who is locally elected every four years. The police belong to the *Helliniki Astinomia (EL.AS)* (Greek Police). Tourist Police can be found in the busier areas of the island.

Customs and Legends

Like all island peoples isolated and kept together for centuries, Rodians still cling strongly to their legends and customs. Although the enormous development of tourism has turned the city of Rodos into a cosmopolitan resort, people in the island villages still stick to their customs and legends and even styles of dresses as a means of self-expression. Some of them are mentioned elsewhere, when we talk about places of interest.

Mythology

According to the myth the first inhabitants of Rodos were the Telchines, brothers of Rodos or Rode, a Nymph, daughter of Poseidon and Halia. These Telchines, well known for their achievements in the fine arts (Statues of Telchinios Apollo at Lindos, Telchinios Hera and Nymphs at Kamiros), in sorcery and in the invention of tools, first settled on Crete and then on Cyprus before coming to Rodos in the middle of the third millenium. The Telchines were succeeded by the Heliades, the descendants of the marriage between Helios and Rodos.

The myths concerning the beginning of Rodos, a dim memory of actual events, are quite numerous. The most popular of them attributes the creation of Rodos to Zeus, in the days when he divided the earth among his fellow gods on Olympus. Helios (the Sun), being absent on the day of the distribution, was not alloted any. When he came back, Zeus suggested reallocating the land, but Helios having seen Rodos glittering beneath the surface of the sea, persuaded the gods to agree that he should be given any part of the world not yet alloted. The gods having agreed, Rodos rose from the sea and Helios made it his bride. This particular myth goes on to mention that Helios had one daughter and seven sons by Rodos, one of whom in turn had three sons, Kamiros, Ialysos and Lindos, who divided the island into three parts, each of them with his own city.

The above mentioned legend, that Helios caused Rodos to arise from the sea, has its origin in fact. Rodos lies on an area which is well known for its many earthquakes through the ages, earthquakes that have caused whole islands to rise from the sea. As a writer quite rightly says: "Lacking geology, the ancients created a myth".

There are many other myths connected with Rodos, all of them having their origin in true historical facts. One of them connects Rodos with Crete and another one connects Rodos with Argos and the Achaeans. Myths are overlapping myths, creating a confusion for the historian, and endless hours of reading enjoyment for the layman.

Actually the name Rodos (ròdon = flower) refers to a rose rather than a nymph. Rodian coins of the fourth, fifth and sixth centuries B.C., having on one face the pomegranate flower are enough evidence that the flower - if any - which gave the island its name was the pomegranate.

above: Rodian coin with the pomegranate flower, emblem of the City.
right: Marble head of Helios, Hellenistic period. Rodos Archaeological Museum.

History

4000-3000 B.C.	Existence of first pre-hellenic tribes on Rodos (Pelasgoi) is claimed by ancient authors and can be proved by the names of the places (Kamiros, Lindos, Ialysos, Atavyris).
1500 B.C.	Establishment of a trading port at the site of Trianda in the N.E. part of the island by Minoan Crete.
1400 B.C.	Mycenean settlements on the whole of the northern part of the island. Minoan Trianda is abandoned.
1300 B.C.	Achaeans from the Argolid settle in Rodos, Kamiros and Ialysos being their biggest settlements.
1183 B.C.	Rodians, under Tlepolemos, leader of the Achaeans, son of Heracles, with a fleet of nine ships take part in the famous "1,000 ships" attack of the Achaeans against Troy.
1150 B.C.	Dorian invasion of Greece.
1100 B.C.	First settlements of Dorians from Argos in Rodos. Lindos, Ialysos and Kamiros become city-states.

The three Rodian cities, the one on Kos and two on the Karian coast (Knidos and Halikarnassos) form the autonomous Dorian *hexapolis* (= six cities). The Rodian cities begin to flourish, take part in commercial exchanges between the East, Attica and Crete, develop once again the long forgotten art of writing. In fact some of the earlier Greek inscriptions were found on Rodos.	700 B.C.
First colonies founded by inhabitants from Lindos: Gela, on the coast of Sicily and Phaselis on the coast of Pamphylia.	690 B.C.
Many Rodian colonies appear in Italy (Naples being one of them), Spain and France. Close relations with Egypt begin.	600 B.C.
Ruler (tyrant) of the city of Lindos is Kleoboulos. Contemporary of Solon, he is included in the list of the seven sages of Ancient Greece. First coins appear in Kamiros.	600-550 B.C.
First attempt of the Persians, under Datis, to conquer Rodos. The Persians break off the siege of Lindos, unable to conquer the city.	491 B.C.
Rodians are compelled to fight with their 40 ships on the Persian side at Salamis.	480 B.C.
Following the victory of the Greeks over the Persians, Rodos is condemned to a period of subjugation to Athens. The three cities of Rodos become members of the 1st Athenian Confederacy and pay tribute.	478/77 B.C.
Diagoras, a Rodian, wins in the 79th Olympic Games. Pindar writes the 7th Olympic Hymn in his honour.	464 B.C.
The second Dorian Hexapolis is founded.	450 B.C.
Outbreak of the Peloponnesian war (431-404 B.C.). The Rodians take at first the part of the Athenians against the Spartans and other Peloponnesians, although they were related ethnically with the latter.	431 B.C.
After the disastrous Sicilian expedition of the Athenians, Rodians revolt against the Confederacy with the Athenians and join the Spartans.	412 B.C.
The city of Rodos is founded, after a consultation among the three ancient cities, Lindos, Kamiros, Ialysos. Helios is declared the God of the city. A new island State is formed along with the islands Chalki, Karpathos, Nisiros, Symi and Tilos. Extensive use of coins.	408 B.C.
Rodos joins the 2nd Athenian Confederacy.	377 B.C.
Rodos joins in an alliance with Thebes against Athens.	363 B.C.
Mausolos, ruler of Karia, succeeds in governing Rodos by establishing an oligarchy that acts as his instrument.	355/54 B.C.
Artemissia, successor to Mausolos, captures Rodos and executes her most important opponents. A plea of the Rodians to the Athenians for help results in Demosthenes delivering his famous speech ''In defence of Rodian freedom'' to no effect. Some years later Rodians manage to free themselves from the Karians.	351 B.C.
Alexander the Great visits Rodos. Rodians align themselves with him. A Macedonian garrison settles in their city.	334 B.C.
Alexandria is founded, with Rodos serving as a model for political organization. A small island off the harbour of Alexandria was called *Antirodos* (rival to Rodos).	331 B.C.
Rodos refuses to take part with Dimitrios Poliorkitis, son of Antigonos the Macedon, in his war against Ptolemy of Egypt and is subjected to one of the most famous sieges of the ancient world. Famous because of the huge size of the besieging force and the modern technical equipment used in the attempt to capture the city. The siege fails and after a year Dimitrios leaves, leaving behind all the siege machines he used.	305/4 B.C.
With the money that the Rodians raised by selling the siege machines that Dimitrios left behind (300 talants), they set up the statue of Helios - the *Colossus of Rodos* - one of the Seven Wonders of the world.	293 B.C.
Rodos fights a successful war against Byzantium. Becomes recognized as the ''Ruler of the Seas'' at this time.	220 B.C.
An earthquake destroys the city's defense walls, houses, dockyards and demolishes the Colossus. The new city built afterwards with generous aid sent by all the rulers and cities of the Hellenistic world, is even finer than it had been before.	227/6 B.C.
Rodos starts cooperating in combatting the enemies of Rome.	201 B.C.
After the defeat of Antiochus III, a large part of Karia and Lykia is ceded to the Rodians.	188 B.C.

The Island and the People

167 B.C.	Rome removes Lykia and almost the whole of Karia from Rodos' control.
166 B.C.	Rome proclaims Delos a free port, a fatal blow to Rodian trade which afterwards declines with dramatic rapidity.
164 B.C.	Alliance between Rodos and Rome.
42 B.C.	Cassius, one of the "tyrannicides" who murdered Caesar, being refused help when he sought it from the Rodians, attacks the island and conquers it. Rodos is stripped of all her money, precious metals, ships and works of art. Her people are butchered and the rest is set to fire.
31 B.C.	Augustus declares Rodos autonomous.
142 A.D.	A great earthquake shakes the island and sinks it back to the status of a provincial city of the Roman empire.
269 A.D.	The Goths raid the island.
297 A.D.	Rodos becomes part of the province of the islands (Provincia Insularum).
4th Century A.D.	With Christianity spreading early to Rodos, it becomes the "Metropolis" of the islands with a number of bishops under its jurisdiction.
515 A.D.	A new earthquake restricts the fortified city to what today is the area of the old city.
620 A.D.	Rodos is raided by the Persians of Khosroes .
653-678 A.D.	The Arabs of Moavia capture the island and sell the ruins of the Colossus.
9th Century A.D.	The Arabs under the Caliph of Baghdad, Arun al Raschid, raid the island.
1089 A.D.	Rodos is captured by the Turkish pirate Tzachas to be freed three years later by the Byzantine fleet.
1097 A.D.	The first Crusaders appear on the island.
1191 A.D.	Richard Coeur de Lion and Philippe of France come to the island for recruits.
1204 A.D.	With the capture of Constantinople by the Crusaders, the governor of Rodos, Leon Gavalas, makes himself independent with the approval of the Venetians.
1248 A.D.	The Genoese gain control of the island, which claims to be independent and only occasionally recognizes the authority of the kingdom of Nicaea.
1309 A.D.	The Knights of St. John, after having been forced out of Jerusalem, after the loss of their previous stronghold at Acre, and after the refusal of the Genoese to let them settle on Rodos, take the island by force, and establish themselves on Rodos. They create an autonomous new state to which the neighbouring islands of Nisiros, Tilos, Simi, Kos, Leros and Kalymnos are added and dominate the island for 213 years.
1480 A.D.	Rodos is besieged by the Turks under the leadership of Meshikh Pasha Palaiologos, a Greek renegade. The resistance of the Rodians and 7,000 knights succeeds in repelling an attacking force of 100,000. After this siege and a subsequent earthquake the knights strengthen more the already existing massive fortifications, which substantially are still the same today.
1522 A.D.	Rodos leading the trade in the Mediterranean is a serious threat to the Turks. Suleiman the Magnificent starts a new siege of the city. On January 1st 1523 the Knights and a large number of Rodians leave the city surrendering it to the Turks. Beginning of the Turkish Rule.
1658 A.D.	Venetian F. Morozini attacks Rodos.
1912 A.D.	Italian army captures Rodos and the rest of the Dodecanese in order to cut Turkish communications with Tripoli, the future aim of Italian colonial expansion.
1943 A.D.	Germans take over the island.
1945-7 A.D.	Rodos is administered by the British.
1947 A.D.	Greek military administration assumes power.
1948, March 1st., A.D.	The Dodecanese are officially incorporated into the Greek State.

Night view of the Palace of the Grand Masters.

Sights and Places of Interest

The Old Town

The **battlements,** 5 km long, surrounding the Old Town are the best introduction to it. Largely the work of Basilio dalla Scuola, they provide excellent views of the old town's mixture of Byzantine, Latin and Turkish architecture.

One can enter the town through its five main gates, the **Marine Gate** (Pyli Navarhiou) and the **Freedom Gate** (Pyli Eleftherias) being the most popular. From these two gates one can reach the **Temple of Aphrodite** (3rd century B.C.), the **Inn of Auvergne** and the **Palace of the Armenia** (Admiralty), the **Museum of Popular Decorative Arts** and the **Byzantine Museum** housed in a 13th c. church.

The **Street of the Knights** (Odos ton Ippoton) was the main street of the medieval Collachium. Restored by the Italians, it is a unique example of a medieval street that has survived till today. The street follows the antique road which led from the port to the Acropolis, now the **Palace of the Grand Masters.** Lined across the street are the **Residences of the Seven Languages.** Entering the Street of the Knights the wall on the left is part of the old **Knight's Hospital** (built between 1440-89), that now houses the **Archaeological Museum.** There you can see finds from the Mycenean to Roman periods, as well as Hellenistic sculptures such as the 3rd c. B.C. **"Anadyomene"** (emerging from the sea) **Aphrodite.** Medieval exhibits can also be seen in the elegant refectory.

Street of the Knights, (Odos ton Ippoton).

9

An archway from the Street of the Knights leads to **Kleovoulos Square** with the reconstructed **Loggia of St. John** and the remains of the Church of St. John which was blown up in the great explosion of 1856.

To the right of the Square is the rebuilt **Palace of the Grand Masters.** Built by Helion de Villeneuve, Grand Master from 1319-46, in imitation of the papal palace at Avignon in his native Provence, to double as a fortress in war and a peacetime residence for the Grand Master and meeting place for senior knights. It was so solid that it suffered remarkably little damage during its many sieges, the final siege of 1522 included. Later on it was used as a prison by the Turks and was wrecked in 1856 by an explosion of gunpowder believed to have been left in the palace vaults since the siege. Intended to be used by Victor Emmanuel III and Mussolini at state visits, the last Italian governor of Rodos (1940), finished building the present passably convincing replica, improved by trees, some ancient mosaic pavements from the island of Kos, and statues, and vases from Lindos. The overall effect is really remarkable although the interior is some way removed from the original and contains some grandiose flights of fancy.

Inside the old town's narrow lanes, darkened by tiled eaves and overhanging wooden balconies, one can spot the 16th c. **Suleiman Mosque** with its added **Venetian portico** and the same Sultan's **hammam** (hot baths) with its distinguished plaster work. On the way down to the lower town one can see on Hippokratous Square the fine 16th c. **Kastellonia,** the Order of St. John's commercial court.

The Ancient City

The remains of the Ancient City cannot rival remains of the same period elsewhere. But knowing that it covered an area which began near the **Temple of Aphrodite** in Simi Square and extended for out to the eastern slope of **Monte Smith** reveals how large the City was. **Monte Smith** (Mt Aghios Stephanos, 110m in height) was named after the British Admiral Sir Sydney Smith who, during Napoleon's war with the Turks, set up an observatory in 1802 watching the French fleet and guarding the Sea of Marmara. It overlooks the 3rd c. B.C. **Stadium** (now restored) and the oddly - shaped **Square Theatre** where classical tragedies are performed in summer. Above the theatre are some columns of the 3rd c.B.C., **Temple of Zeus, Temple of Athena Polias** and rather more of the **Temple of Apollo.**

The New Town

First settled by Greeks who were not allowed to stay within the wall of the old town at night when the Turks occupied Rodos. The **Mandraki Harbour** with its mole with three windmills and Fort St. Nicholas, a cylindrical tower dating from 1464-67, is now used as a yacht anchorage. Dominating the harbour mouth is the **Church of Evangelismos** (Annunciation), b. 1925, a replica of the destroyed church of St. John in the Old City. The **Fountain** outside its west end is a copy of the Fontana Grande of Viterbo.

The modern New Town is primarily Italian. Many villas, hospitals, public buildings - including the **Town Hall, Government House**, the **Aquarium** and the **New Market,** an octagonal arcaded building with an open market in the centre - were built between 1912 and the last war. The only picturesque and not Italian building outside the old Town is the **Mourad Reis Mosque** (b. 1523) surrounded by derelict Turkish tombs.

Sights near the city

3 km from Rodos is the vast **Rodini Park,** a pretty wooded area on either side of a ravine, with winding paths, streams and pools, water lilies and grottoes, where the Wine Festival is held annually.Ruins of an **aqueduct,** probably Roman, and of a Hellenistic funeral monument, inaccurately called the **Tomb of the Ptolemies,** can be seen next to Rodini Park.

above: General view of the Palace of the Grand Masters.
below: The imposing entrance of the Palace.

11

The Island and the People

above: The Mandraki harbour.
below: The Aghios Fanourios Str., one of the oldest in the Old City.

The East Coast

56 km from the city of Rodos lies **Lindos** now a small village of 1,000 inhab., chief of the three ancient cities before the foundation of Rodos and the most important place in the island after Rodos itself in the Middle Ages. The place was settled in the 3rd millenium B.C. and a temple to Athena existed from at least the 10th c. B.C. Its geographical position between two harbours and its Acropolis rising to a height of 114 m made it the most important of the three ancient cities of Rodos. The Acropolis itself was restored by the Italians before 1938.

On the way to the Acropolis of Lindos up a long stairway, we pass by the ruined 27-tier **Theatre.** Passing under the outer gate we come to a terrace with Timocharis' colossal (4.5m × 5m) **carved relief of a ship and its captain** (Hellenistic trireme), which served as the base of a statue of a priest of Poseidon called Aghesandros. To the right of the relief are the remains of the ancient **Sacred Way.** A long staircase leads to the main gate and a vaulted passage above which is a medieval chamber which formed part of the **Governor's Palace.** Once inside the massive walls of the Acropolis you can see the 5th c. B.C. **Doric Stoa,** 20 of the 42 columns of which have been re-erected. From the Stoa a monumental staircase leads to a higher terrace with foundations of the **Propylaia** (b. after 407 B.C.) and after that at the edge of the cliff stands the small but elegant 4th c. B.C. **Doric Temple of Athena Lindia** rebuilt after a fire in 348 B.C. The Knights used the sanctuary as a quarry for their impressive 15th c. castle, but enough was left for a restrained reconstruction by the Italians.

above: The Doric Stoa. below: Timocharis' ship.

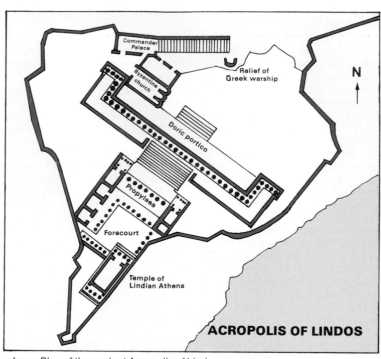

Commander Palace

Byzantine church

Relief of Greek warship

N

Doric portico

Propylaea

Forecourt

Temple of Lindian Athena

ACROPOLIS OF LINDOS

above: Plan of the ancient Acropolis of Lindos.
below: General view of Lindos.

The West Coast

At **Ialysos** (Filerimos) there is the 18th c. **Church of the Dormition** (Kimissis Theotokou) with a beautifully carved **ikonostasion**. 8 km inland is the site of the ancient Ialysos. The **Acropolis of Ialysos** - one of the three ancient cities of Rodos - commands a splendid view over the island and the sea. On the Acropolis remain the foundations of a 3rd c. B.C. **Temple of Athena Ialysia** on which stands the **baptismal font** of a 5th c. church. Imposing, restored in 1931 and given a new tower, is the Knight's church of **Our Lady of Filerimos** with Catholic and Orthodox altars. Above is the restored **Monastery,** from which a path leads to the ruined castle of the Knights. Lower down are a restored 4th c. **Doric Fountain** and the **Necropolis** with Late Mycenean, Geometric, Archaic and Classical cemeteries.

7 km off the 18 km mark of the west side main road is the **Valley of Butterflies** (Petaloudhes). It is a narrow valley, 1.5 km long, where rustic bridges cross brooks shaded by enormous plane trees. Between July   August clouds of golden moths fill the air and settle on the amber orientalis trees.

Further south (34 km) are the remains of another of the ancient cities, **Kamiros.** It was rediscovered in 1859 and excavated in 1929. The city had neither fortifications nor acropolis. An impressive 3rd C. BC **Doric Stoa** has been reconstructed near the foundations of the **Temple of Athena.**

above: The Knights' Church of Our Lady of Filerimos.
below: The remains of Ancient Kamiros.

above: The breathtaking view from the castle of Monolithos, near the small village of Siana on the West coast. below: the hot springs at Kallithea.

HOTELS IN RODOS

GENERAL NOTES

CLASSIFICATION: Standards of accomodation, classification and minimum prices are set by the Government (National Tourist Organization of Greece). Hotels are classified as: **De Luxe (L), A, B, C, D** and **E** category.
This classification roughly corresponds to the star classification system used in Great Britain and in Europe.

PRICES: As mentioned above prices are set by the Government. Actually the Government sets the minimum prices per hotel category with no ceiling as to what the maximum could be. You are advised to check the prices beforehand so that unpleasant surprises can be avoided.

Notes:

1) Service charge (15%) is included in the prices.
2) V.A.T. stamp duty, city or community taxes are not included.
3) The legal charges for central heating / air conditioning are usually, though not always, included in room prices.
4) A single person occupying a double room is charged 80% of the double room rate.
5) An extra bed in a room-only at the client's request - will increase the room rate by 20%.
6) The room rates are applicable daily up to 12.00 noon of the following day. Stay till 6 p.m. is charged for an extra half-day. Beyond 6 p.m. the charge is as for a full day.
7) An increase of 10% may be added to room rates for a stay of two days or less.
8) The room rates of hotels located in summer holidays areas, may be increased by 15% during the period July 1st to September 15th.
9) In all rooms a price chart is displayed giving full details of applicable charges.
10) Many hotels grant special rates for groups upon request, particularly during the low season.

The Hotels Owners Association of Rhodes is at your entire disposal for any information you may require concerning the hotels and their prices, as well as for reservations.

Example of a Hotel Entry

Telephone and Telex number

Classification ➡ (A) BLUE BAY HOTEL AND APARTMENTS ↓
Address ➡ Ialyssos Ave.-Ialyssos **Tel.** 0241/92352, 91131
851 00 RHODES **Tlx.** 292300 PABA GR
Open: Mar. - Nov.

Additional Information ➡ Located on a natural, smooth, private beach, about 10 km from the town of Rhodes, the Blue Bay Complex provides all the facilities for a restful vacation by the sea.

Accomodation and Facilities Symbols **rm** 322/**b** 644
(Key to Symbols and Abbreviations page 70)

C.C. American Express

* Most hotels will accept credit cards, as this is indicated in the relevant entry. Traveller's cheques issued by banks are accepted almost everywhere. In most, if not all, of the hotels you can pay in foreign currency but be careful with the exchange rates that are used!

★ De luxe
GRAND HOTEL ASTIR PALACE
1 Akti Miaouli str.
851 00 RHODES

Tel. 0241/26284-9
Tlx. 292 121 GHSP GR
Open: Jan. - Dec.

rm 378/**b** 700

De Luxe
MIRAMARE BEACH
Ixia
851 00 RHODES

Tel. 0241/24251-3
Tlx. 922123 MIRA GR
Open: Apr. - Oct.

Luxury bungalows resort set amidst well tended gardens with numerous trees. Situated close to a 1000 m long beach. All bungalows have sea view. It boasts of a plano bar next to a swimming pool in tropical setting. Restaurant serves delicious specialities.

rm 179/**b** 330

C.C. No

★ De Luxe
OLYMPIC PALACE HOTEL
Ialyssos Ave.
Ixia
851 00 RHODES

Tel. 0241/28775
Tlx. 292263
Open: Jan. - Dec.

rm 333/**b** 591

★ De Luxe
RODOS PALACE HOTEL
Ialyssos Ave.
Ixia
851 00 RHODES

Tel. 0241/25222-20
26222-20
Tlx. 292212 Rprc Gr
Open: Jan. - Dec.

rm 610/**b** 1220

★ A´ APOLLO BEACH HOTEL
Faliraki
851 00 RHODES

Tel. 0241/85251, 85513
Tlx. 292220
Open: Apr. - Oct.

rm 293/**b** 539

★ A´ APOLLONIA HOTEL APARTMENTS
Ialyssos Ave.-Ixia
851 00 RHODES

Tel. 0241/92951
Open: Jan. - Dec.

rm 17/**b** 34

A´ AVRA BEACH HOTEL
Ialyssos Ave.-Ixia
851 00 RHODES

Tel. 0241/25284, 25308
Tlx. 214
Open: Apr. - Oct.

Surrounded by a big garden, it's located 6 km from the town of Rhodes. Small shopping center, kid's swimming pool, kindergarten, hairdresser, rent a car, restaurant, bar, open bar, disco etc.

rm 125/**b** 231
bung. 61/**b** 122

C.C. No

★ A´ BEL AIR HOTEL
Ialyssos Ave.-Ixia
851 00 RHODES

Tel. 0241/23711-4
Open: Apr. - Oct.

rm 158/**b** 293

A´ BELVEDERE HOTEL
P.O. Box 144
851 00 RHODES

Tel. 0241/24471-4
Tlx. 292120 BERO GR
Open: Apr. - Oct.

Hotel Belvedere is situated in an ideal location on the coast of the Aegean sea, just a short walk to the town's centre. 165 tastefully furnished rooms with bath/shower, balcony, private beach with umbrellas, deckchairs and showers, bar and Greek and International cuisine restaurant.

rm 212/**b** 394

C.C. Diners, Amer. Express, Visa, Emb orokarta,
Ethnokarta, Barcley's

A´ BLUE BAY HOTEL AND APARTMENTS
Ialyssos Ave.-Ialyssos
851 00 RHODES

Tel. 0241/92352, 91131
Tlx. 292300 PABA GR
Open: Mar. - Nov.

Located on a natural, smooth, private beach, about 10 km from the town of Rhodes, the Blue Bay Complex provides all the facilities for a restful vacation by the sea.

rm 322/**b** 644

C.C. American Express

A´ BLUE HORIZON HOTEL
Trianda
851 00 RHODES

Tel.0241/93479-86
Tlx. 292381
Open: Apr. - Oct.

A brand new hotel located on the coast of Ialyssos. 221 hotel rooms, bungalows and suites each one with terrace or balcony, bathroom, telephone and radio. Snack-bar, swimming pool, children's pool and play - ground, cozy bar and taverna.

rm 151/**b** 292, **bung** 60/**b** 120

C.C. American Express, Diners

★ A´ BLUE SEA HOTEL
Faliraki
851 00 RHODES

Tel. 0241/29271, 85512
Tlx. 292241
Open: Jan. - Dec.

rm 296/**b** 548

A´ BLUE SKY HOTEL
Platia Psaropoulas
P.O. Box 144
851 00 RHODES

Tel. 0241/24091-2-3
Tlx. 292160 BLSK GR
Open: Apr. - Nov.

Right on the sea front, only five minutes walk from the town centre. All 182 bedrooms have central heating, telephone, three channel music, private bathroom and balcony and any have a splendid sea view. Also shops, airdresser, banquetting hall and night club ive music-Greek shows).

rm 182/b 370

.C. American Express

A´ CAIRO PALACE HOTEL
8 Eth. Makariou str.   Tel. 0241/27600, 24328
851 00 RHODES   Open: Apr. - Oct.
m 111/b 201

A´ CALYPSO HOTEL   Tel. 0241/85622, 85455
Faliraki   Tlx. 292356
851 00 RHODES   Open: Apr. - Oct.

On the sandy beach of Faliraki, professionally decorated and fully airconditioned with igh standard of service and a friendly atmosphere, Calypso Hotel offers: children's wimming pool and playground, tennis courts, minigolf, beach facilities, beauty salon, conference room, cards room, billiards, T.V. and video theatre, shopping centre and a lot more.

m 259/b 479

.C. American Express

★ A´ CARAVEL HOTEL APARTMENTS
Ixia   Tel. 0241/21843
851 00 RHODES
rm 23/b 46

A´ CHEVALIER'S PALACE HOTEL
3 G. Griva str.   Tel. 0241/21360, 21411
851 00 RHODES   Tlx. 292163
        Open: Jan. - Dec.

We meet our clients at airport / harbour on request; special service for newly married, V.I.P. etc.; public relations and information office; meetings, small congress and manifestations hall available. Also Greek open air evenings, films and competitions (chess, bridge, darts, ping-pong etc.). Reduced terms in winter.

m 188/b 368

.C. American Express, Diners

A´ COLOSSOS BEACH CLUB HOTEL
P.O. Box 105-Faliraki   Tel. 0241/85502
851 00 RHODES   Tlx. 292291 CLUB GR
        Open: Apr. - Oct.

Newly built hotel, directly on the sandy beach of Faliraki, 9 km from the town of Rhodes. 3 swimming pools, children's playground, 4 tennis courts, mini-golf, cocktail bar, 3 bars, restaurant, taverna, self-service, cafeteria, disco, super market, shops, congress rooms and more.

m 408/b 746
Bung. 108/216

.C. No

★ A´ DESPINA PENSION   Tel: 0241/51248
Golf Area - Afandou
851 00 RHODES

b 18

A´ DIONYSSOS HOTEL   Tel. 0241/23021
Faneromeni-Ixia   Tlx. 292151
851 00 RHODES   Open: Apr. - Oct.

Situated 200 m from the sea. 140 apartments with two beds, living room, 2 divans, kitchenette with refrigerator, bathroom, telephone and music. 150 rooms with two beds and divan, bathroom, telephone, music, refrigerator. 2 swimming pools, 2 bars, snack bar, drugstore, sauna, 2 tennis courts, mini-golf and hairdresser.

rm 281/b 523

C.C. American Express, Diners

A´ DORETA BEACH HOTEL
P.O. Box 131-Theologos   Tel. 0241/41441-3
851 00 RHODES   Tlx. 292305 DOR GR
        Open: 1st Apr. - 30th Oct.

The Doreta Beach Hotel, framed by extensive gardens, stands on a gently sloping sand and pebble beach only 15 km from the town of Rhodes. Offers 24 hour full entertainment programme.

rm 285/b 546
bung. 34/68 b

C.C. Diners, American Express, Access

A´ EDEN ROC HOTEL   Tel. 0241/23851, 23859
P.O. Box 203   Tlx. 292116
Reni Koskinou   Open: Apr. - Oct.
851 00 RHODES

In the eastern part of the island, only 5 km from the town of Rhodes, the Eden Roc Hotel stands right on the water's edge, surrounded by big gardens. It offers: sea-skiing, bicycling, windsurfing, 2 big tennis courts, sauna and massage.

rm 258/b 712
bung. 115/b 712

C.C. American Express, Ethnokarta

★ A´ ELAFOS-ELAFINA HOTEL
Profitis Elias   Tel. 0241/21221-3
851 00 RHODES   01/3243961
        Tlx. 292121 GHSP GR
        Open: May. - Oct.

rm 68/b 127

A´ ELECTRA PALACE   Tel. 0241/92521
Paralia Ialyssou - Trianda   Open: Apr. - Oct.
851 00 RHODES
The Electra Palace belongs to a chain of luxurious hotels and is situated amidst a picturesque setting on the lovely coast of Trianda. It is designed to meet the exacting de-

mands of discriminating pleasure seekers and offers full relaxation, fun, glamour and excitement.

rm 215/b 402

C.C. American Express, Carte Blanche, Ethnokarta

A´ ELINA HOTEL
P.O. Box 31, Ixia
851 00 RHODES

Tel. 0241/92944-5
Tlx. 0292264 AEGEV
Open: Apr. - Oct.

Extremely convenient location in a private beach, 8 km away and easily reached by frequent local bus service to Rhodes. High-standard food in both International and Greek cuisine with choice of menu. Most bedrooms have a nice sea - view.

rm 150/b 277

C.C. Diners, American Express

A´ ELISABETH HOTEL APARTMENTS
P.O Box 441
851 00 RHODES

Tel. 0241/92681, 92491
Tlx. 292295
Open: Apr. - Oct.

Surrounded by a wonderful garden it is the ideal resort place for families. Facilities include private beach with sun umbrellas, special children's swimming pool, grill-snack, tennis court, disco, open air bar, shopping arcade, gift shop, library, card room, spacious lobbies and TV room.

apt. 100

C.C. American Express, Ethnokarta, Emborokarta

★ A´ ESPERIDES HOTEL
P.O. Box 202
Faliraki
851 00 RHODES

Tel. 0241/85503,
85547
Tlx. 292223 ESRH GR
Open: Apr. - Oct.

Dominating the heart of Faliraki bay, just 13 km from the town of Rhodes, surrounded by a vast garden lawn and recreation areas, lies "Esperides Beach Hotel" a large modern complex especially recommended for families. Three swimming pools. All rooms with telephone and radio and fridge. Restaurant, cocktail bar, terrace lounge, bridge room, T.V. room, tavern, snack bar, discoteque, supermarket, hairdressing salon, rent-a-car / bicycle office, children's playground.

rm 550/b 1016

A´ ESPEROS PALACE HOTEL
P.O. Box 202
Faliraki
851 00 RHODES

Tel. 0241/85742-5
Tlx: 292353 ESRH GR
Open: Apr. - Oct.

A new modern hotel located on the best beach of the island, near "Esperides Beach Hotel" of the same company. All rooms with bathroom, balcony, sea view, music, automatic self-dialling telephone system with wake-up mode and a small fridge. Main restaurant, snack bar and main bar all with large verandas overlooking to the pool and the beach. Games room, tourist shop, swimming pool and sandy beach are part of the facilities offered.

rm 178/b 366

A´ EVA APARTMENTS
22 Ir. Polytechniou str.
851 00 RHODES

Tel. 0241/29508
Tlx. 292120 BERO GR
(For Aparthotel Eva)
Open: Apr. - Oct.

A´ Class furnished apartments in the centre of the town, 5 minutes from the beach. One-/two bedrooms each, lounge, telephone, bathroom, equipped kitchen, hall, verandas, spacious bar, amenities within easy reach. We promise our clientele an agreeable stay.

rm 18/b 33

C.C. No

A´ FALIRAKI BEACH HOTEL
P.O. Box 104
851 00 RHODES

Tel. 0241/26511, 85301
Tlx. 292219
Open: Mar. - Nov.

A first class hotel, directly on the sandy beach near Faliraki village, 5 km from the Golf Course. 300 air-conditioned rooms, restaurant, taverna, bar, disco, TV room, supermarket, hairdresser, tennis courts, swimming pools, playground, water-sports, room-service and baby sitting. Special prices: Mar. - Apr. - May - Oct.

rm 300/b 600
bung. 4/b 12

C.C. All

★ A´ FILERIMOS HOTEL APARTMENTS
37 Ialyssou-Kremasti Ave.
851 00 RHODES

Tel. 0241/29510,
29933
Open: Jan. - Dec.

rm 81/b 162

★ A´ GOLDEN BEACH HOTEL
Akti Ialyssou-Ixia
851 00 RHODES

Tel. 0241/92411-5
Tlx. 292155 GLDB GR
Open: Apr. - Oct.

rm 225/b 431

★ A´ HELIOS PALACE
   HOTEL APARTMENTS
5 Dragoumi str.
851 00 RHODES

Tel. 0241/27709
Open: Apr. - Oct.

rm 34/b 64

✱ A´ IALYSSOS BAY HOTEL
Ialyssos
851 00 RHODES
Tel. 0241/91841-5
Open: Apr. - Oct.

rm 153/**b** 282

C.C. No

A´ IBISCUS HOTEL
P.O. Box 90-17 Nisirou str.
851 00 RHODES
Tel. 0241/23321-2-3
Tlx. 292131
Open: Mar - Nov.

A friendly, modern hotel, standing just across the road from the sandy beach, which can also be reached by an underpass. Terrace, bar lounge, two additional lounges, dining-room, TV-room, card tables and a steak house.

rm 207/**b** 383

C.C. American Express, Diners

✱ A´ IMPERIAL HOTEL
23 V.Konstantinou str.
851 00 RHODES
Tel. 0241/22431-2
Open: Apr. - Oct.

rm 81/**b** 151

✱ A´ ISAIAS HOTEL APARTMENTS
8 Patr. Athinagora str.
851 00 RHODES
Tel. 0241/29263
Open: Jan. - Dec.

rm 26/**b** 40

✱ A´ KAMIROS HOTEL
1 25th March str.
851 00 RHODES
Tel. 0241/22591-3
Open: Mar. - Oct.

rm 48/**b** 90

C.C. American Express, Diners, Visa

A´ LINDOS BAY HOTEL
Lindos
851 00 RHODES
Tel. 0241/42210-1-2
Tlx. 292311
Open: 15th Apr. - 30th Oct.

Built on the most beautiful beach of the island, 42 km from the town of Rhodes and 3.5 km from Lindos, it combines relaxation and the opportunity to visit Lindos, the place where many civilizations left their marks. Among other facilities it offers all summer sports in a crystal-clear sea.

rm 192/**b** 372

C.C. American Express

A´ MEDITERRANEAN HOTEL
35-37 Kos str.
851 00 RHODES
Tel. 0241/24661-5
Tlx. 292108 BAK GR
Open: Mar. - Nov.

An elegant, distinguished hotel, situated on the best sandy beach of Rhodes, only two minutes walk from the town centre. The entire hotel is beautifully designed and decorated. There are spacious lounges, bar and dining room.

rm 154/**b** 292

C.C. Eurocard, Access, American Express, Visa, Diners

A´ METROPOLITAN CAPSIS HOTEL
Ixia
851 00 RHODES
Tel. 0241/25015
Tlx. 292 185
Open: Apr. - Oct.

Two fully equipped conference halls (300 persons each), full animation programme (aerobics - video - shows - Greek nights - games - events etc.) and a nursery station for up to six year old children. Additionally, indoor swimming pool, shopping arcade, cards room, sauna, massage and fast-food restaurant.

rm 644/**b** 1198
bung. 45/**b** 90

C.C. American Express, Diners, Master's, Visa, Carte Blanche, Ethnokarta, Emborokarta

✱ A´ MONTE SMITH (HOTEL) APARTMENTS
Rodopoula
851 00 RHODES
Tel. 0241/29540, 27078
Open: Jan. - Dec.

rm 18/**b** 36

✱ A´ OASIS HOLIDAYS HOTEL BUNGALOWS
Afandou
851 00 RHODES
Tel. 0241/51359
Open: Apr. - Oct.

rm 37/**b** 70

A´ OCEANIS HOTEL
P.O. Box 31-Ixia
851 00 RHODES
Tel. 0241/24881, 24886
Tlx. 292132 OCEA GR
Open: Apr. - Oct.

Extremely convenient location on a private beach, 8 km away and easily reached by frequent local bus service to Rhodes. High-standard food in both International and Greek cuisine with choice of menu. Most bedrooms have a nice sea-view.

rm 219/**b** 432

C.C. Diners Club, American Express, Ethnokarta

A´ PARADISE HOTEL
Reni Koskinou
851 00 RHODES
Tel. 0241/82484, 29220
Tlx. 292174 PARA GR
Open: Apr. - Oct.

Situated on the eastern part of the island, 6 km from the town of Rhodes in the area of Kallithea, it offers among other things conference facilities for over 600 people.

rm 630/**b** 1200

C.C. All.

A´ PARK HOTEL
Tel. 0241/24611-2

Hotels in Rodos

12 R. Fereou str.
P.O. Box 105
851 00 RHODES
Tlx. 292137 PARK GR
Open: Apr. - Oct.

Situated on the best and most peaceful residential side of the town, and yet only a few minutes walk from the sandy beach. All rooms modernly decorated; restaurant, bar, ample halls and lounge, verandas, gardens and a big swimming pool.

rm 90/**b** 170
C.C. No

★ A´ PEGASOS HOTEL
Faliraki
851 00 RHODES
Tel. 0241/85331
Tlx. 292 241
Open: Mar. - Nov.

b 450

★ A´ POSSIDONIA HOTEL APARTMENTS
Ialyssos Ave.-Ixia
851 00 RHODES
Tel. 0241/222276
Open: Jan. - Dec.

rm 34/**b** 68

A´ REGINA HOTEL
20 E.Makariou
P.O. Box 20
851 00 RHODES
Tel. 0241/22171-4
Tlx. 292140 ZUV GR
Open: Apr. - Oct.

rm 82/**b** 150

C.C. No

★ A´ RIVIERA HOTEL
2 Akti Miaouli
851 00 RHODES
Tel. 0241/22581-2, 24801
Open: Jan. - Dec.

rm 62/**b** 116

★ A´ RODOS BAY HOTEL
Ixia
851 00 RHODES
Tel. 0241/23661-5
Tlx. 292150 Rbay Gr.
Open: Apr. - Oct.

rm 330/**b** 611

A´ RODOS BEACH HOTEL
Faliraki
851 00 RHODES
Tel. 0241/29261
Tlx. 292358 ROBE GE
Open: Mar. - Nov.

This large sea-front hotel is set amidst big gardens full of trees. It also offers 81 tastefully furnished bungalows.

rm 236/**bung.** 81/**b** 500

C.C. Diners, American Express

★ A´ SIRAVAST HOTEL
Platia Vasileos Pavlou
851 00 RHODES
Tel. 0241/23551-7
Tlx. 292154 JET GR
Open: Apr. - Dec.

rm 92/**b** 170

A´ SIRENE BEACH HOTEL
Kritika
851 00 RHODES
Tel. 0241/30638
Tlx. 292404 SIRE GR
Open: Apr. - Oct.

The Sirene Beach Hotel also disposes of T.V. lounge, kiosk and children's swimming pool.

rm 100/**b** 200
C.C. No

A´ STEPS OF LINDOS HOTEL
P.O. Box 179
851 00 RHODES
Tel. 0241/42263-7
Tlx. 292 352
Open: Apr. - Oct.

A perfect choice for a quiet, relaxing holiday. Built in a whitewashed village style in a lovely position on a hillside with superb view over a long, sandy beach. Freshwater swimming pool, children's pool, poolside bar, two comfortable lounges and bars, dining room, adjoining terraces with fine sea view, games room, floodlit tennis court, table tennis, children's playground, mini golf.

rm 320/**b** 620

C.C. Diners, Visa, American Express, Emborokarta, Ethnokarta.

A´ SUN BEACH APARTMENTS HOTEL
Ialyssos
851 00 RHODES
Tel. 0241/91920, 93470
Tlx. 292395 SUBE GR
Open: Apr. - Oct.

A new building on the beautiful beach of Ialyssos with cosy atmosphere and special programmes and games for children, 9 km from Rhodes town, on the way to the airport. 85 well furnished apartments, 70 with seaview.

rm 85/**b** 176

C.C. American Express

★ A´ SUN PALACE HOTEL
Faliraki
851 00 RHODES
Tel. 0241/85650
Open: Apr. - Oct.

rm 200

A´ SUNWING HOTEL
Kallithea
851 00 RHODES
Tel. 0241/28600-6
Tlx. 292252
Open: Apr. - Oct.

Sea-front hotel, 4 km from the town of Rhodes. It offers a large restaurant overlooking the pool and the sea, beach, taverna, cocktail bar, grill terrace with dancing, shows and entertainment. Sport facilities include two tennis courts, mini golf, swimming pool, volley ball etc. "Sunwing" offers comfort, relaxation and entertainment in an international atmosphere.

rm 298/**b** 692
bung. 91/**b** 182

C.C. American Express, Diners, Visa, EURO Card, Master's, Access, Ethnokarta.

A´ VERINO APARTHOTEL
52 Griva str.
Tel. 0241/22625

851 00 RHODES   **Open:** Apr. - Oct.

Situated 300 m from the best beach of Rhodes. Every apartment with a large veranda.

rm 12/**b** 24

C.C. Visa, Diners, American Express, Master's

B´ ACANDIA HOTEL   **Tel.** 0241/22251-4
6 I. Polytechniou str.   **Open:** Apr. - Oct.
851 00 RHODES

Situated close to the famous beach of Rhodes and also very near to the centre of the town. 82 modernly furnished bedrooms, all with private bath - balcony - telephone - radio. Luxurious restaurant and bar with beautiful veranda and TV room.

rm 82/**b** 160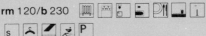

C.C. No

B´ AGLAIA HOTEL   **Tel.** 0241/22061-2
35 Apol. Amerikis str.   **Tlx.** 292370
851 00 RHODES   **Open:** Mar. - Nov.

Directly on the beach, only 10 minutes walk from the town centre. Comfortable rooms with private shower/bath, tel., central heating, balcony, piped music, most of them overlooking the sea. Family-run hotel with efficient staff always available to ensure a comfortable stay.

rm 120/**b** 230

C.C. Diners, Visa, American Express

★ B´ ALEXANDROS APARTMENTS
21 Ag. Georgiou str.   **Tel.** 0241/20023
851 00 RHODES   **Open:** Jan. - Dec.

rm 19/**b** 38

B´ ALEXIA HOTEL   **Tel.** 0241/24061-3
54 Orfanidou str.   **Open:** Apr. - Oct.
851 00 RHODES

Suitable for independent people who want to discover the town for themselves, and yet to have a comfortable and relaxing base to return to.

rm 135/**b** 257

C.C. No

B´ ALIA APARTMENTS   **Tel.** 0241/31410
Ialyssos Ave.-Ixia   **Open:** Apr. - Oct.
851 00 RHODES

Furnished apartments, with 2 beds and two divans in the living room, bathroom and fully-equipped kitchenette. Can accomodate up to 4 persons.

rm 12/**b** 24

C.C. No

★ B´ AMPHITHEATER APARTMENTS
421 A. Theatrou - Lindos   **Open:** Apr. - Oct.
851 00 RHODES

b 22

C.C. No

★ B´ AMPHITRION HOTEL   **Tel.** 0241/26880, 20121
8-10 A. Diakou str.
851 00 RHODES   **Open:** Apr. - Oct.

rm 101/**b** 220

C.C. No

B´ ANGELA HOTEL   **Tel.** 0241/24614, 24014
7 28 Octovriou str.   **Open:** Apr. - Oct.
851 00 RHODES

Hotel Angela is located very near to the beach and a few minutes walk from the town centre. All rooms with music, telephone and balcony. Bar, spacious lounges moderny furnished, breakfast lounge, sun-bathing space on 6th floor, special prices for groups.

rm 64/**b** 118
C.C. No

B´ AQUARIUS APARTMENTS
19 Lohagou Fanouraki str.   **Tel.** 0241/28107
851 00 RHODES   **Open:** Apr. - Oct.

rm 20/**b** 75
C.C. No

B´ ATHINA HOTEL   **Tel.** 0241/22634, 22631
27 G. Leon str.   **Tlx.** 292168 COST GR
Neochorion   **Open:** Apr. - Oct.
851 00 RHODES

A luxurious B´ Class hotel just 80 m from the sea. All rooms equipped with private shower/bath, central heating, telephone, music and balcony. Large swimming pool, bar and solarium.

rm 142/**b** 267

C.C. American Express, Master Charge

★ B´ BELLA VISTA HOTEL   **Tel.** 0241/29900
Akti Miaouli & Tilou str.   **Open:** May.-Dec.
851 00 RHODES

rm 32/**b** 54

★ B´ CACTUS HOTEL   **Tel.** 0241/26100, 26088
14 Kos str.   **Tlx.** 292235 NICI GR
851 00 RHODES   **Open:** Jan. - Dec.

rm 177/**b** 336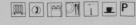

★ B´ CONSTANTINOS HOTEL
65 Amerikis str.   **Tel.** 0241/22971, 24758
851 00 RHODES   **Tlx.** 292117 GRNS GR
    Open: Jan. - Dec.

rm 133/**b** 246

B´ CONTINENTAL HOTEL
8 Ag. Ioannou str.   **Tel.** 0241/30897, 30885
851 00 RHODES   **Open:** Mar. - Oct.

Situated on a quiet part of Rhodes, 5 minutes from the old town and 10 minutes from the sea. Comfortable rooms, personal service, guaranteed cleanliness and warm at-

mosphere.
rm 11'3/**b** 219

C.C. No

★ B´ CORALI HOTEL
85 V.Konstantinou &
Patmou str.
851 00 RHODES
Tel. 0241/24911-2
Open: Mar. - Nov

rm 115/**b** 217

★ B´ DELFINI HOTEL
45 Ethn. Makariou str.
851 00 RHODES
Tel. 0241/24691-3
Open: Apr. - Oct.

rm 70/**b** 135

B´ DESPO HOTEL
40 Vas. Sofias str.
851 00 RHODES
Tel. 0241/22571-3,
30519
Open: Jan. - Dec.

Situated in the town centre, no more than 3 min. walk from the beach. Big and comfortable breakfast lounge. Central heating throughout winter time.

rm 64/**b** 122

C.C. American Express, Visa, Diners

B´ ERODIA HOTEL APARTMENTS
7 Kritis str., P.O. Box 2
851 00 RHODES
Tel. 0241/31361, 34741
Open: Apr. - Oct.

A very modern hotel (built 1982) located in the tourist centre of Rhodes, only 150 meters from the seashore.It combines quietness, comfortable residence and perfect service in a homely atmosphere. Cafeteria, bar, TV room in the ground floor, solarium in the terrace.

apt. 15/**b** 34
C.C. No

B´ ESPERIA HOTEL
7 G. Grica str.
851 00 RHODES
Tel. 0241/23941-3
Tlx. 292223
Open: Apr. - Nov.

Right in the centre of the town, very close to the Casino and only 100 m from the beach, Esperia Hotel was built in 1966 and was completely modernized in 1982. Among other facilities it offers T.V. room, bridge room and information room.

rm 191/**b** 364

C.C. American Express

★ B´ EUROPA HOTEL
94 28 Octovriou str.
851 00 RHODES
Tel. 0241/22711, 24810
Open: Jan. - Oct.

rm 80/**b** 147

★ B´ GEORGE HOTEL APARTMENTS
49 Papalouka str.
851 00 RHODES
Tel. 0241/21964
Open: Apr. - Oct.

rm 12/**b** 24

★ B´ INTEUROPA APARTMENTS
Kastellorizou str.
851 00 RHODES
Tel. 0241/25042

b 40

B´ JOLLY GUEST HOUSE
36 Loh. Phanouraki str.
851 00 RHODES
Tel. 0241/25425

300 yards from the beach and 3 min. walk to the commercial centre of the town. All rooms equipped with refrigerator, electric cooker, telephone, music and shower. Garden with bar where you can enjoy a nice cold drink. Lift to all rooms.

rm 16/**b** 28

C.C. Visa

★ B´ LEFKA HOTEL APARTMENTS
184 Ialyssos Ave.
851 00 RHODES
Tel. 0241/23511

rm 13/**b** 21

B´ LITO HOTEL
Triadon Ave.-Ixia
851 00 RHODES
Tel. 0241/23511-2
Open: Apr. - Oct.

Located in Ixia, one of the most beautiful areas of the island, and only 3 km from the town of Rhodes. Convenient bus service all day long. Built on the water's edge with a private beach. It's very near to the local shopping centre.

rm 97/**b** 184
C.C. No

B´ LOMENIZ HOTEL
Cl. Peper - Constadini str.
851 00 RHODES
Tel. 0241/34649
Tlx. 292 360 LOME GR
Open: Apr. - Oct.

Newly-build hotel with 400 beds situated on the quiet sandy beach "Zefyros", with swimming-pool, bar, taverna, garden, table tennis, billiard, modern rooms with large balconies. The warm surrounding helps to make your stay enjoyable. The hotel is only five minutes away from the centre of the city.

b 400

B´ MANOUSOS HOTEL
20-22 G. Leon, P.O.Box 92
851 00 RHODES
Tel. 0241/22741-4
Tlx. 292219
Open: Jan. - Dec.

Situated near the town centre, only a minute's walk from the sandy beach and the Casino, "Manousos Hotel" offers: 130 comfortable rooms, restaurant, bar, TV room, 24 hour baby sitting and room service, hairdresser's, super market and shops. Reduced terms in winter.

rm 130/**b** 260

C.C. American Express, Carte Blanche, Access, Ethnokarta.

★ B´ MOUSES HOTEL BUNGALOWS
Faliraki
851 00 RHODES
Tel. 0241/85303
Open: Apr. - Oct.

rm 29/**b** 58

★ B´ OASSIS HOTEL
Tel. 0241/24177

16-18,25 Martiou str.
851 00 RHODES

rm 12/**b** 30

* B´ OLYMPIC HOTEL   Tel. 0241/24311-2
12 Platia V. Pavlou   Open: Apr. - Oct.
851 00 RHODES

rm 46/**b** 86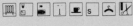

* B´ PAHOS HOTEL APARTMENTS
Ialyssos Ave.-Ialyssos   Tel. 0241/92611
85100 RHODES

rm 21/**b** 44

B´ PHOENIX (PALM) HOTEL
2 Ex.Panteleimonos str.   Tel. 0241/24531-3
851 00 RHODES   Open: Apr. - Oct.

Palm Hotel is located in the town of Rhodes, 6 min. walk from the centre and 25 m from the beach.

rm 80/**b** 143
C.C. No

B´ PLAZA HOTEL   Tel. 0241/22501-5
7 Ierou Lohou str.   Tlx. 292129
851 00 RHODES   Open: Jan. - Dec.

10% discount offered to airline companies employees and to commercial representatives.

rm 128/**b** 244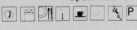
C.C. American Express, Diners, Visa, Masters, Access, Emborokarta, Ethnokarta.

* B´ POSEIDON HOTEL   Tel. 0241/24541-2
Kritika   Open: May. - Oct.
851 00 RHODES

rm 35/**b** 63

* B´ SANDY COAST HOTEL APARTMENTS
5 Konstantinidi str.   Tel. 0241/26697, 22240
851 00 RHODES   Tlx. 292243
                         Open: Mar. - Oct.

rm 18/**b** 36

* B´ SOLEMAR HOTEL   Tel. 0241/82941-2
66 Sotiros str.-Ixia   Open: Mar. - Oct.
851 00 RHODES

rm 102/**b** 194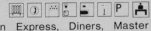

B´ SPARTALIS HOTEL   Tel. 0241/24371-2
2 N. Plastira str.   Open: Jan. - Dec.
851 00 RHODES

Situated in the centre of the town, facing the picturesque port of Mandraki. Television lounge. Special prices in winter.

rm 79/**b** 141
C.C. American Express, Diners, Master Charge, Ethnokarta

B´ STELLA GUEST HOUSE   Tel. 0241/24935
58 Dilveraki str.   Open: Apr. - Oct.
851 00 RHODES

Charming and friendly, this small guest house is run by resident proprietors. Situated in the centre of the modern part of the town "Stella" is about ten minutes walk from the fascinating old town of Rhodes and a few minutes stroll from the nearest beach.

rm 12/**b** 26
C.C. No

* B´ SUNRISE HOTEL APARTMENTS
18 Akti Miaouli str.   Tel. 0241/30009, 22944
851 00 RHODES   Open: Jan. - Dec.

rm 12/**b** 24

* B´ THERMAE HOTEL   Tel. 0241/24351-4
2 Dimokratias str.   Tlx. 292127
851 00 RHODES   Open: Apr. - Oct.

rm 118/**b** 210

B´ VIOLETTA HOTEL APARTMENTS
Faliraki   Tel. 0241/85501
851 00 RHODES   Open: Apr. - Oct.

Just 300 m from Faliraki Beach, on the Rhodes-Lindos Ave., Violetta Hotel is surrounded by gardens full of flowers and trees. All rooms have two balconies, one viewing the sea and the other viewing the fields and the mountain.

rm 13/**b** 26
C.C. No

* B´ WING APARTMENTS   Tel. 0241/32361
Ixia   Open: Apr. - Oct.
851 00 RHODES

b 18

B´ "XENIA" GOLF   Tel. 0241/51121-33
Afandou   Open: Apr. - Oct.
851 00 RHODES

Built on the magnificent beach of Afandou it's 18 km from the town of Rhodes on the way to Lindos. 52 beds (26 rooms), restaurant, bar and three swimming pools with full amenities operating on the golf course grounds during golf tournaments.

rm 26/**b** 52

C.C. Diners, Ethnokarta

C´ ACHILLION HOTEL   Tel. 0241/24604-5
14 Platia Vas. Pavlou   Open: Jan.-Dec.
851 00 RHODES

Completely modernized in 1982.

rm 49/**b** 86
C.C. No

* C´ ADONIS HOTEL   Tel. 0241/27791
7 V.Konstantinou str.   Open: Mar. - Nov.
851 00 RHODES

rm 15/**b** 26

C´ AEGEON HOTEL   Tel. 0241/22492, 22491
3 Er. Stavrou str.   Open: Apr. - Oct.
851 00 RHODES

Located near the town centre and yet only

Hotels in Rodos

100 m from the sea, "Aegeon Hotel" offers a pleasant and homely atmosphere. All rooms with sea-view.

rm 15/b 28

C.C. No

C' AEGLI HOTEL
Tel. 0241/22789, 24659
90 Kolokotroni str.
Open: Apr. - Oct.
851 00 RHONIS

Situated in the centre of the new town only 5 minutes walk from the beach. Newly built and luxuriously furnished with all modern comforts. All 40 bedrooms with private shower/bath, telephone and balcony. Spacious lounge, lift and Bar.

rm 37/b 69

C.C. No

C' AFRICA HOTEL
Tel. 0241724645, 24979
63 Al. Diakou str.
Open: Apr. - Oct.
851 00 RHODES

Situated in the entrance of the town, five minutes from the business centre and just 60 meters from the beach. All rooms with bath-shower, telephone and balcony. Have a nice time in the pleasant atmosphere of our Bar, Lounge and veranda.

rm 75/b 144

C.C. No

C' ALS HOTEL
Tel. 0241/22481-2
10 V. Pavlou str.
Open: Apr. - Oct.
851 00 RHODES

Located in the heart of the town on the magnificent one hundred - palm - trees - square. "Als" Hotel is only 300 meters from the commercial centre and 100 meters from the sea. Noted for its homely atmosphere, delicious breakfast and well maintained premises.

rm 52/b 95

C.C. No

★ C' AMARYLLIS HOTEL
Tel. 0241/24522
44 Othonos & Amalias str.
Open: Apr. - Dec.
851 00 RHODES

rm 39/b 75

★ C' AMAZONA HOTEL
Tel. 0241/34523
Kallithea Ave.
851 00 RHODES

b 54

★ C' AMBASSADEUR HOTEL
Tel. 0241/24679
53 Othonos & Amalias str.
Open: Apr. - Oct.
851 00 RHODES

rm 42/b 80

C' ANTHOULA PENSION
Tel. 0241/24052
46 Alex. Diakou str.
Open: Jan. - Dec.
851 00 RHODES

rm 12/b 24

C.C. No

★C' APHRODITI (VENUS) HOTEL
50 Othonos & Amalias str.
Tel. 0241/24668
851 00 RHODES
Open: Mar. - Oct.

rm 55/b 101

★ C' ARION HOTEL
Tel. 0241/20004, 20006
17 Eth. Makariou str.
Open: Mar. - Oct.
851 00 RHODES

rm 47/b 82

C' ASTORIA HOTEL
Tel. 0241/27482,
39 Vas. Sofias str.
24804-5
851 00 RHODES
Open: Apr. - Oct.

Reduced prices (20% and over) offered from Apr. 1st to Jun. 6th each year for groups of more than 4 persons.

rm 38/b 72
C.C. No

C' ASTRON HOTEL
Tel. 0241/24651, 28995
10 J. Kazouli str.
Open: Apr. - Oct.
851 00 RHODES

New hotel with 43 bedrooms within easy walking distance from beach and town. Bar, Lounge, lift to all floors and pleasant terrace. All bedrooms with private shower, toilet and 220 Volt shaver. Central heating, telephone and balcony in all rooms.

rm 43/b 82
C.C. American Express

★ C' ATHINEA PENSION
Tel. 0241/23221
45 Pythagora str.
Open: Jan. - Dec.
Palea Agora
851 00 RHODES

rm 8/b 16

★ C' ATLANTIS HOTEL
Tel. 0241/24821-2
29 I. Dragoumi str.
Open: Mar. - Nov.
851 00 RHODES

rm 47/b 84

★ C' BILLY'S APTS
Tel. 0241/85567
Faliraki
851 00 RHODES

b 36

★ C' BOUCAINVILLEA HOTEL
20, 28 Octovriou str.
Tel. 0241/34303
851 00 RHODES

b 20

★ C' CARACAS HOTEL
Tel. 0241/22371-2
19 Th. Sofouli str.
Open: Apr. - Oct.
851 00 RHODES

A quiet and fiendly resort place, 500 m from the sea and a 5 min. walk from the centre of the town.

rm 52/b 99
C.C. No

★ C' CARINA HOTEL
Tel. 0241/22381-2
56 Stratigou Griva str.
Open: May. - Oct.
851 00 RHODES

rm 59/b 108

★ C´ CONGO HOTEL
145 Dendrinou str.
851 00 RHODES

Tel. 0241/24023
Open: Apr. - Oct.

rm 36/b 57

★ C´ DIANA HOTEL **Tel.** 0241/24677, 28967
68 G.Griva str. **Open:** Mar. - Oct.
851 00 RHODES

rm 42/b 82

★ C´ DIETHNES HOTEL **Tel.** 0241/30221, 24595
12 Ioan.Kazouli str. **Open:** Apr. - Oct.
851 00 RHODES

rm 42/b 78
C.C. No

★ C´ DIMITRA HOTEL **Tel.** 0241/85309, 85254
Faliraki **Open:** Mar. - Dec.
851 00 RHODES

rm 38/b 73

C´ EDELWEISS HOTEL **Tel.** 0241/85305, 85442
Faliraki **Open:** Apr.-Dec.
851 00 RHODES

Built in no more than 100 m from the beach,
"Edelweiss Hotel" is surrounded by shops,
restaurants, and banks.

rm 57/b 102
C.C. No

★ C´ EL GRECO HOTEL **Tel.** 0241/24071-2
2 G. Efstathiou str. **Open:** Jan. - Dec.
851 00 RHODES

rm 75/b 140

★ C´ ELITE HOTEL **Tel.** 0241/22391, 20961
15 Ex. Panteleimonos str. **Open:** Mar. - Oct.
851 00 RHODES

rm 45/b 86

★ C´ EMBONA HOTEL **Tel.** 0241/24139
61 G. Griva str. **Open:** May - Sept.
851 00 RHODES

rm 16/b 30

★ C´ EVI HOTEL **Tel.** 0241/85586
Faliraki **Open:** Jan. - Dec.
851 00 RHODES

rm 57/b 110

C´ FLORA HOTEL **Tel.** 0241/24538, 26130
13 28 Octovriou str. **Open:** Apr. - Oct.
851 00 RHODES

The hotel is situated in the centre of the
town, 200 meters from the sea.

rm 98/b 188
C.C. No

★ C´ FLORIDA HOTEL **Tel.** 0241/22111, 26843
5 Amarantou str. **Open:** Jan. - Dec.
851 00 RHODES
rm 19/b 36

★ C´ FOUR SEASONS HOTEL
32 Akti Miaouli str. **Tel.** 0241/22340
851 00 RHODES **Open:** Apr. - Oct.

rm 27/b 51

★ C´ FOTINI HOTEL **Tel.** 0241/29131
32 Anth. Zervou str.
851 00 RHODES

b 24

★ C´ GALATIA PENSION **Tel.** 0241/22659
2 Erythrou Stavrou str. **Open:** Jan. - Dec.
851 00 RHODES

rm 10/b 20

C´ GALAXIAS HOTEL **Tel.** 0241/29203, 22401
72 An. Marias str. **Open:** Apr. - Oct.
851 00 RHODES

rm 37/b 71
C.C. No

C´ GREEN - VIEW HOTEL
5 Kremastis Ave. **Tel.** 0241/91010, 91009
Ialyssos **Open:** June - Oct.
851 00 RHODES

A newly built hotel, located between the
town of Rhodes and the airport, on Ialyssos
Kremasti Avenue, near a shopping centre,
with frequent bus and taxi service. All bed
rooms with telephone, music, private
shower and balcony. Also bar, TV room and
garage.

rm 32/b 64
C.C. No

C´ HELENA HOTEL **Tel.** 0241/22681, 24755
78 G. Griva str. **Open:** Mar. - Oct.
851 00 RHODES

rm 83/b 163
C.C. No

★ C´ HERMES HOTEL **Tel.** 0241/27677
5 N. Plastira str. **Open:** Jan. - Dec.
851 00 RHODES

rm 35/b 64

★ C´ IATRIDES APTS **Tel.** 0241/85315
Faliraki
851 00 RHODES

b 19

C´ IDEAL HOTEL APARTMENTS
Faliraki **Tel.** 0241/85518
851 00 RHODES **Open:** Apr. - Oct.

Family-run hotel apartments enterprise,
200 m from the sandy beach and 13 km from
the town of Rhodes. Each apartment with kitchenette, refrigerator, bathroom with shower,
balcony.

rm 19/b 44
C.C. No

★ C´ ILIOVASSILEMA HOTEL
Theologos **Tel.** 0241/41201
851 00 RHODES **Open:** Apr. - Oct.

Hotels in Rodos

rm 9/**b** 18

rm 16/**b** 32

★ C´ IMPALA APARTMENTS Tel. 0241/29704
72 Parodos Kanada str. **Open:** May - Oct.
851 00 RHODES

★ C´ IRENE HOTEL Tel. 0241/24761-2
9 25 Martiou str. **Open:** Apr. - Dec.
851 00 RHODES

rm 56/**b** 101

★ C´ ISABELLA HOTEL Tel. 0241/22651
12 Ammochostou str. **Open:** Jan. - Dec.
851 00 RHODES

rm 42/**b** 76

★ C´ KARMEN APTS Tel. 0241/30357
65 Alex. Diakou str.
851 00 RHODES

b 13

C´ KYPRIOTIS HOTEL Tel. 0241/32861, 32521
2 Valaoritou str. **Open:** Apr. - Oct.
851 00 RHODES

A new and modern hotel set on the beautiful beach of "Psaropoula". Pleasant cocktail bar, snack bar, mini-market, swimming pool, games room, TV - video lounge.

rm 163/**b** 324

★ C´ LIA PENSION Tel. 0241/20371, 26209
66 c Pythagora str. **Open:** Jan. - Dec.
851 00 RHODES

rm 7/**b** 16

★ C´ LIDO HOTEL Tel. 0241/85226
P.O.Box 363 **Open:** Apr. - Oct.
Faliraki
851 00 RHODES

rm 20/**b** 38

C.C. No

C´ LISA GUEST HOUSE
Ialyssos Tel. 0241/92181, 93557
851 00 RHODES **Open:** Apr. - Oct.

Big, sunny rooms, each with a big balcony. A quiet and peaceful resort place ideal for relaxation. Greenery surroundings, quick and efficient service, warm and friendly atmosphere.

rm 60/**b** 111

C.C. No

★ C´ LYDIA HOTEL Tel. 0241/22871-2
31 25 Martiou str. **Open:** Jan. - Dec.
851 00 RHODES

rm 26/**b** 53

★ C´ MAJESTIC HOTEL Tel. 0241/22031-3
A. Zervou str. **Open:** Mar. - Dec.
851 00 RHODES

rm 79/**b** 147

★ C´ MANDRAKI HOTEL Tel. 0241/25693,

39 D. Theodoraki str. 23431
851 00 RHODES Tlx. 292102

rm 8/**b** 20

★ C´ MANIAS APTS Tel. 0241/85379
Faliraki
851 00 RHODES

b 55

C´ MARIE HOTEL Tel. 0241/30577
7 Kos str. (5 lines)
851 00 RHODES Tlx. 292313 MARI GR
Open: Apr. - Nov.

With heated swimming-pool & saunas "Marie" is proud of its reputation of offering luxury in C´ class prices. 125 rooms each with balcony, bathroom, telephone, music. It is facing the town's park and it's located 100 m from the beach. Bar - TV Lounge - Pub - Cafeteria - Gelateria - Super Market.

rm 125/**b** 235

C.C. No

★ C´ MARIETTE HOTEL APARTMENTS
30 Th. Sofouli str. Tel. 0241/34593
851 00 RHODES Tlx. 292313 MARI GR
Open: 10th Apr. 31th Oct.

"Mariette" Hotel-Apartments offers to its guests 22 fully furnished apartments, all with private balcony, toilette, telephone and radio. Friendly and quiet atmosphere, pleasant and unforgettable stay.

rm 22/**b** 55

C.C. No

★ C´ MASSARI PENSION Tel. 0241/22469
42 Herodotou str. **Open:** Jan. - Dec.
851 00 RHODES

rm 10/**b** 22

★ C´ MATSOUKARIS APTS Tel. 0241/91277
6 Diagoridon str.
Kremasti
851 00 RHODES

b 16

★ C´ MIMOSA HOTEL Tel. 0241/24026, 20432
4 G. Efstathiou str. **Open:** Apr. - Oct.
851 00 RHODES

rm 71/**b** 117

★ C´ MINOS HOTEL Tel. 0241/24041, 20291
8 Alex. Diakou str. **Open:** Apr. - Oct.
851 00 RHODES

rm 72/**b** 133

C´ MOSCHOS HOTEL Tel. 0241/25983, 24764
5 Eth. Dodecanision str. **Open:** 1st Apr.-5th Nov.
851 00 RHODES

Very near the business centre and only a hundred meters from the beach "Moschos Hotel" is built in a quiet little street away from traffic noises, offering a warm and homely atmosphere. Very low prices and children under eight free for Apr. - May, June - Oct.

rm 34/**b** 64

C.C. No

★ C´ NAFSIKA HOTEL Tel. 0241/21996
8 Par. Syl. U.S.A. str. Open: Apr. - Oct.
851 00 RHODES

rm 40/**b** 70

★ C´ NEW YORK HOTEL Tel. 0241/22481
36 Ionos Dragoumi str. Open: Apr. - Oct.
851 00 RHODES

rm 28/**b** 49

★ C´ NOUFARA HOTEL Tel. 0241/24545
35 V. Sophias str. Open: Mar. - Oct.
851 00 RHODES

rm 49/**b** 86

★ C´ ORION APTS Tel. 0241/35338
V. Nikitara str.
851 00 RHODES

b 40

★ C´ PALLADION HOTEL Tel. 0241/24054
20 Dilberaki str.
851 00 RHODES

b 24

★ C´ PARTHENON HOTEL Tel. 0241/22351-2
Anthoulas Zervou Open: Mar. - Oct.
P.O. Box 68
851 00 RHODES

rm 79/**b** 150

★ C´ PAVLIDIS HOTEL Tel. 0241/20281, 28677
15 28 Octovriou str. Open: Apr. - Oct.
851 00 RHODES

rm 50/**b** 96

C´ PEARL HOTEL Tel. 0241/22420-1
15 G. Griva str. Open: Apr. - Nov.
851 00 RHODES

rm 38/**b** 70

C.C. No

★ C´ PHAEDRA HOTEL Tel. 0241/24207, 22791
7 Arcadiou str. Open: Jan. - Dec.
851 00 RHODES

rm 62/**b** 120

★ C´ PETALOUDA HOTEL Tel. 0241/24207
49 Ammochostou str. Open: Jan. - Dec.
851 00 RHODES

rm 39/**b** 75

★ C´ ROMA HOTEL Tel. 0241/24447, 23821
Ixia Open: Apr. - Oct.
851 00 RHODES

rm 43/**b** 80

★ C´ ROYAL HOTEL Tel. 0241/24601-2
50 V. Sophias str. Open: Jan. - Dec.
851 00 RHODES

rm 60/**b** 108

★ C´ SAINT ANTONIO HOTEL Tel. 0241/24971
7 Ionos Dragoumi str. Open: Apr. - Oct.
851 00 RHODES

rm 43/**b** 82

★ C´ SANTA MARIA HOTEL Tel. 0241/21343
5-7 I. Dragoumi str.
851 00 RHODES

b 43

★ C´ SARONIS HOTEL Tel. 0241/22811-2
51 Othonos & Amalias str. Open: Jan. - Dec.
851 00 RHODES

rm 28/**b** 54

C´ SAVOY HOTEL
9 Eth. Dodecanission str. Tel. 0241/20721-2
851 00 RHODES Open: Jan. - Dec.

In the centre of the town.

rm 47/**b** 87

C´ SEMIRAMIS HOTEL Tel. 0241/20741-4
18 I. Metaxa str. Open: Mar. - Nov.
851 00 RHODES

Situated 700 m from the centre of the town and only 100 m from the beach.

rm 120/**b** 230

C.C. No

★ C´ SOLEIL HOTEL Tel. 0241/24190, 24290
2 Democratias str. Open: Jul. - Sept.
851 00 RHODES

rm 90/**b** 160

★ C´ SOPHIA HOTEL Tel. 0241/85423, 85218
Faliraki Open: May - Oct.
851 00 RHODES

rm 29/**b** 56

★ C´ SUNNY APARTMENTS Tel. 0241/22968
Akti Kanari
851 00 RHODES

b 28

★ C´ SYLVIA HOTEL Tel. 024122551-2
114 Kolokotroni str. Open: Jan. - Dec.
851 00 RHODES

rm 39/**b** 71

C´ THOLOS HOTEL-APARTMENTS
Theologos Tel. 0241/41583
851 00 RHODES Open: Jan. - Dec.

"Tholos Hotel" is situated in the village of Theologos, 22 km from the town of Rhodes, near the road to Ancient Kamiros. Furnished apartments, pleasant surroundings and an excellent service promise unforgettable vacations. (Kitchenette with refrigerator).

rm 18/**b** 36
C.C. No

C´ TILOS HOTEL Tel. 0241/24591, 24991
49 Makariou str. Open: 15th Mar. - 15th Nov.

29

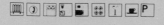

851 00 RHODES

Located in the centre of the town "Tilos Hotel" offers friendly service in a warm, homely atmosphere.

rm 21/b 39

C.C. No

* C´ VASSILIA HOTEL Tel. 0241/24051
55 Othonos & Amalias str. Open: Jan. - Dec.

rm 41/b 77

C´ VELLOIS HOTEL Tel. 0241/26241, 24615
Ixia Open: May - Oct.
851 00 RHODES

rm 51/b 92

C.C. No

* C´ VICTORIA HOTEL Tel. 0241/24626
22 25 Martiou str. Open: Apr. - Oct.
851 00 RHODES

rm 35/b 66

C´ VILLA HELENA (APARTMENTS)
Dimokratias Ave.-Paradissi Tel. 0241/91243,
851 06 RHODES 92915
 Open: Apr. - Nov.

Situated in the small town of Paradissi, 15 km from the town of Rhodes, 1 km from the International Airport. Luxuriously built, surrounded by a big garden. Each apartment with kitchenette (electric cooker - refrigerator) can accomodate 2-4 persons.

rm 10/b 20

C.C. No

* C´ VILLA RHODOS Tel. 0241/20614
36 G. Leom str. Open: Jan. - Dec.
Neochorion
851 00 RHODES

rm 27/b 53

C´ ZEUS PENSION Tel. 0241/23129
72 Ag. Nicolaou str. Open: 15th Mar. - 31st Dec.

Surrounded by a big garden. Efficient and friendly service.

rm 9/b 19

C.C. No

* D´ ALKYON HOTEL Tel. 0241/24344
15-17 Kos str. Open: Apr. - Oct.
851 00 RHODES

rm 18/b 35

* D´ ANASTASSIA HOTEL
16 28 Octovriou str. Tel. 0241/21815, 28007
Neochorion Open: Jan. - Dec.
851 00 RHODES

rm 9/b 24

* D´ ARCHANGELOS HOTEL
184 7th Martiou str. Te:. 0241/21230, 22230
Archagelos Open: Jan. - Dec.
851 00 RHODES

rm 19/b 37

* D´ ARIETTE HOTEL Tel. 0241/22490
41 Apol. Rodiou str. Open: Mar. - Nov.
851 00 RHODES

rm 21/b 39

* D´ ATLAS HOTEL Tel. 0241/24022, 25773
44 Orfanidou & Kritis str. Open: Apr. - Oct.
851 00 RHODES

rm 18/b 33

* D´ D'OR HOTEL Tel. 0241/22911
81 Orfanidou str. Open: Jan. - Dec.
851 00 RHODES

rm 16/b 25

* D´ EFROSSINI HOTEL Tel. 0241/24629
32a Apol. Rodiou str.
851 00 RHODES

rm 13/b 29

D´ FIVOS HOTEL Tel. 0241/22600
Archangelos Open: Apr. - Oct.
851 00 RHODES

On the edge of Archangelos village a new modern building, with a 3-acre garden, very quiet and friendly resort place. The village is famous for its artistic handicrafts, jewellery, embroidery and some of the best beaches of the island.

rm 12/b 26

C.C. No

* D´ IRIS HOTEL Tel. 0241/27343
31 Kritis & Orfanidou str. Open: Apr. - Oct.
851 00 RHODES

rm 16/b 30

* D´ PANTHEON HOTEL Tel. 0241/24557
11 Tarpon Springs str. Open: Jan. - Dec.
851 00 RHODES

rm 20/b 35

C.C. No

* D´ PARIS HOTEL Tel. 0241/26356
88 Ag. Fanouriou str. Open: Apr. - Dec.
851 00 RHODES

rm 18/b 34

* D´ PHAEDRA HOTEL Tel. 0241/44218
Lardos Open: Jan. - Dec.
851 00 RHODES

rm 10/b 21

D´ REX HOTEL Tel. 0241/22620
18b Papalouka str. Open: Jan. - Dec.
851 00 RHODES

100 m from the beach and only 300 m from the town centre. "Rex Hotel" is set in a very quiet and peaceful place, full of trees.

rm 27/b 51

C.C. No

* D´ RHODIAKON HOTEL Tel. 0241/22051-2

20 Apol. Amerikis str.   **Open:** Jan. - Dec.
851 00 RHODES

rm 21/**b** 39   P

★ D´ RODINI HOTEL   Tel. 0241/27814, 20628
42 Lindou str.   **Open:** Mar. - Dec.
851 00 RHODES

rm 30/**b** 55   [icons]
P

D´ STAR HOTEL   **Tel.** 0241/22853
129 Dendrinou str.   **Open:** Jan. - Dec.
851 00 RHODES

  1.500 m. from the centre of the town, 150 m from the beach. Central heating, snack bar, lounge with music and TV. Friendly and homely athmosphere.

rm 20/**b** 36   [icons] P
C.C. No

★ D´ XANTHI HOTEL   **Tel.** 0241/24996
18 Papalouka str.   **Open:** Jan. - Dec.
851 00 RHODES

rm 18/**b** 34

★ D´ ZEFYROS HOTEL   **Tel.** 0241/22826
135 Dendrinou str.   **Open:** Jan. - Dec.
851 00 RHODES

rm 16/**b** 25   [icons]

★ E´ CABANA HOTEL   **Tel.** 0241/84543
Faliraki   **Open:** Mar. - Nov.
851 00 RHODES

rm 20/**b** 38   [icons] P
C.C. No

★ E´ COVA BEACH HOTEL
11 Kanada str.   **Tel.** 0241/26877, 26413
851 00 RHODES   **Open:** Jan. - Dec.

rm 9/**b** 18   [icons] P

★ E´ CRITI HOTEL   **Tel.** 0241/21341
35 Kanada str.   **Open:** Jan. - Dec.
Aghios Nikolaos
851 00 RHODES

rm 12/**b** 27   P

★ E´ EFKALYPTOS HOTEL   Tel: 0241/51432
Kolymbia
Afandou
851 00 RHODES

b 19

★ E´ FALIRON HOTEL   **Tel.** 0241/85483
Faliraki   **Open:** Apr. - Oct.
851 00 RHODES

rm 17/**b** 33

★ E´ FIESTA HOTEL   **Tel.** 0241/85498
Faliraki
851 00 RHODES

rm 26/**b** 57

★ E´ IALYSSOS HOTEL   **Tel.** 0241/28556-7
63 Orfanidou str.   **Open:** Apr. - Oct.

851 00 RHODES

rm 18/**b** 33   P

★ E´ JOHANNES HOTEL Tel.0241/51655,51565
Afandou   **Open:** Apr. - Oct.
851 00 RHODES

rm 20/**b** 41

★ E´ KASTRO HOTEL   **Tel.** 0241/20446
14 Arionos str.   **Open:** Jan. - Dec.
851 00 RHODES

rm 10/**b** 21   P

E´ LA LUNA HOTEL   **Tel.** 0241/25856
21 lerokleous str.   **Open:** Jan. - Dec.
851 00 RHODES

  A very quiet place, situated in the centre of the old town of Rhodes, surrounded by a beatiful garden.

rm 7/**b** 18   [icons]
C.C. No

E´ MARGET HOTEL   **Tel.** 0241/25289
12 A. Korai str.   **Open:** Mar. - Oct.
851 00 RHODES

  Newly-built E´ class hotel, modernly furnished, just 10 min. walk from the centre of the town. 18 rooms, each with balcony and private bath, 100 m from the best beach of Rhodes. Mini-bar, breakfast e.t.c.

rm 18/**b** 39   [icons] P
C.C. No

★ E´ MARINA HOTEL   **Tel.** 0241/28589
5 P. Rodiou str.   **Open:** Jan. Dec.
851 00 RHODES

rm 13/**b** 32

★ E´ MARNIN HOTEL   **Tel.** 0241/27494
Oth.-Am. & Amarantou str.   **Open:** Mar. - Nov.
851 00 RHODES

rm 18/**b** 37

★ E´ MATSIS HOTEL   **Tel.** 0241/91064
1 Lykourgou str.   **Open:** Apr. - Oct.
851 00 RHODES

rm 12/**b** 22

★ E´ MOURATIS HOTEL   **Tel.** 0241/42260
Kalathos
851 00 RHODES

b 28

★ E´ NEW VILLAGE INN HOTEL
10 Konstantinopaidos str.   Tel: 0241/34947
851 00 RHODES

b 32

★ E´ NEST (FOLIA) HOTEL   **Tel.** 0241/85581
Faliraki
851 00 RHODES

b 12

★ E´ ODYSIA HOTEL   Tel: 0241/85288
Faliraki

ANTIQUITIES (EXPORT)

Antiquities may be exported only with the approval of the Archaeological Service and the Greek Ministry of Culture and Sciences. Lawbreakers may face a stiff fine and/or a prison sentence of up to five years. So, before you buy check with: Archaeological Service: Platia Argirokastrou, tel: 27674

AIR SCHEDULES (DOMESTIC)

Day	Dep	Arr	Flt No.	AirCt	Day	Dep	Arr	Flt No.	AirCt
From ATHENS					**To ATHENS**				
DLY	0515	0610	OA700	AB3N	DLY	0710	0805	OA701	AB3
»	0915	1010	OA702	707	»	1130	1215	OA703	707
»	1630	1725	OA706	707	»	1805	1900	OA707	707
	exc.	WED,	FRI		»	exc.	WED,	FRI	
	1910	2005	OA708	727		2045	2140	OA709	727
»	2100	2155	OA714	707	»	2235	2330	OA715	707
WED	1700	1755	OA335	727	WED	2210	2305	OA336	727
»	1910	2005	OA710	727	THU	0030	0125	OA711	727N
FRI	1910	2005	OA710	727	SAT	0030	0125	OA711	727N
From HERAKLION					**To HERAKLION**				
DLY	2030	2110	OA520	737	DLY	2150	2230	OA521	737
From KARPATHOS					**To KARPATHOS**				
DLY	1700	1745	OA095	D08	DLY	1555	1640	OA094	D08
»	1920	2005	OA097	D08	»	1815	1900	OA096	D08
MON	1030	1115	OA091	D08	MON	0925	1010	OA090	D08
»	1250	1335	OA093	D08	»	1145	1230	OA092	D08
TUE	1250	1335	OA087	D08	TUE	0925	1010	OA086	D08
WED	1030	1115	OA091	D08	WED	0925	1010	OA090	D08
»	1250	1335	OA093	D08	»	1145	1230	OA092	D08
THU	1250	1335	OA087	D08	THU	0925	1010	OA086	D08
FRI	1030	1115	OA091	D08	FRI	0925	1010	OA090	D08
»	1250	1335	OA093	D08	»	1145	1230	OA092	D08
SAT	1250	1335	OA089	D08	SAT	0925	1010	OA088	D08
SUN	1250	1335	OA089	D08	SUN	0925	1010	OA088	D08
From KASSOS					**To KASSOS**				
MON	0810	0855	OA085	D08	MON	0805	0750	OA084	D08
WED	0810	0855	OA085	D08	WED	0705	0750	OA084	D08
FRI	0810	0855	OA085	D08	FRI	0705	0750	OA084	D08
SUN	0810	0855	OA085	D08	SUN	0705	0750	OA084	D08
From KASTELORIZO					**To KASTELORIZO**				
THU	1110	1155	OA027	D08	THU	1005	1050	OA026	D08
SUN	1110	1155	OA027	D08	SUN	1005	1050	OA026	D08
From KOS					**To KOS**				
DLY	1455	1525	OA021	D08	DLY	1405	1435	OA020	D08
From LEROS					**To LEROS**				
MON	1245	1410	OA019	SHS	TUE	1105	1225	OA018	SHS
WED	1245	1410	OA019	SHS	THU	1105	1225	OA018	SHS
FRI	1245	1410	OA019	SHS	SAT	1105	1225	OA018	SHS
SAT	1245	1410	OA019	SHS					
From MYKONOS					**To MYKONOS**				
MON	1310	1420	OA524	SH3	MON	1440	1550	OA525	SH3
TUE	0840	1040	OA528	SH3	TUE	1100	1300	OA529	SH3
WED	1310	1420	OA524	SH3	WED	1440	1550	OA525	SH3
THU	0840	1040	OA528	SH3	THU	1100	1300	OA529	SH3
FRI	1310	1420	OA524	SH3	FRI	1440	1550	OA525	SH3
SAT	0840	1040	OA528	SH3	SAT	1100	1300	OA529	SH3
SUN	1310	1420	OA524	SH3	SUN	1440	1550	OA525	SH3
From PAROS					**To PAROS**				
TUE	0835	0945	OA014	D08	TUE	1215	1325	OA015	D08
THU	0835	0945	OA014	D08	THU	1215	1325	OA015	D08
SAT	0835	0945	OA014	D08	SAT	1215	1325	OA015	D08
SUN	0835	0945	OA014	D08	SUN	1215	1325	OA015	D08
From SANTORINI					**To SANTORINI**				
TUE	0940	1040	OA528	SH3	TUE	1100	1200	OA529	SH3
THU	0940	1040	OA528	SH3	THU	1100	1200	OA529	SH3
SAT	0940	1040	OA528	SH3	SAT	1100	1200	OA529	SH3
From SITIA					**To SITIA**				
TUE	0800	0855	OA083	D08	TUE	0615	0740	OA082	D08
THU	0800	0855	OA083	D08	THU	0615	0740	OA082	D08
SAT	0800	0855	OA083	D08	SAT	0615	0740	OA082	D08
From THESSALONIKI					**To THESSALONIKI**				
WED	2240	2350	OA561	727	WED	2045	2200	OA560	727
FRI	2240	2350	OA561	727	FRI	2045	2200	OA560	727

Types of Aircraft
AB3: A 300B Airbus
D08: Dornier 228
SH3: Shorts 330
SHS: Skyran
707: Boeing 707
727: Boeing 727
737: Boeing 737

BANKS

Bank of Crete
Akademias Square
Tel. 0241-23546

Bank of Piraeus
29, Grigori Lambraki Str.
Tel. 0241-20286

Commercial Bank of Greece
30, Kyprou Square
Tel. 0241-27688

Credit Bank
46, Tarpon Springs Str.
Tel. 0241-28851

General Bank of Greece
Amerikis - G. Efstathiou Str.
Tel. 0241-23903

Ionian and Popular Bank of Greece
Kyprou Square
Tel. 0241-24121

National Bank of Greece
Kyprou Square
Tel. 0241-27031

Banking Hours;
Monday - Thursday: 08.00-14.00
Friday: 08.00-13.30

Some banks may be open in the mornings of Saturdays, Sundays and public holidays but only for currency exhange transactions.

BATHING

What makes Rodos so popular among tourists is the combination of a fine climate, interesting sightseeing combining ancient, medieval and modern history, and the fine beaches surrounding the city of Rodos and extending to the western part of the island for more than 20 km. No matter where you stay, the nearest beach shouldn't be more than a 10 minute walk.

In some of the beaches you will be required to pay a small fee for the chairs and the sun-shades (umbrellas) that will be provided for you.

BICYCLE AND MOTORSCOOTER RENTAL

There are many rental agencies scattered around Rodos city centre.
Here are some of these agencies:
ALFA 5, 28 Octovriou Str. Tel: 0241-20253

DELPHI 8, Anthoulas Zervou Str. Tel: 0241-23923, -34102

MANIAS 51, Orfanidou Str. Tel: 0241-20225

MOTOMOVE 3, Pl. Plassa Str. Tel: 0241-27827

RENT HIRE 7, John Kazouli Str. Tel: 0241-28676

RENT NEW 13, Griva Str. Tel: 0241-27142

PILOT 4, Kritis Str. Tel: 0241-32285

STATIS 22, V. Constantinou Str. Tel: 0241-21292

BOATS and FERRIES

Most of the ships sailing from Piraeus to Rodos are ferries that can carry quite a few cars, among them your own if you wish! The trip lasts roughly 20-22 hours. Rodos is connected with virtually all the main islands of the Aegean sea and some of the Eastern Mediterranean, with departures that vary from once per week to once per day.

Agencies for tickets and information

OMIROS (F/B)	Red Sea Agency,	Tel: 0241-27721, -22683
KYKLADES (F/B)	Kydon Agency,	Tel: 0241-23000
KAMIROS (F/B)	D.A.N.E. Agency,	Tel: 0241-30930
PANORMITIS	Zervos Agency,	Tel: 0241-22308
SOL PHRYNE (C/F)		Tel: 01-452.9991
SOL OLYMPIA II		Tel: 01-452.9991

BUSES

In general there is a reliable, well-organized bus service.

Buses for the East Coast (the entrance of "Sound and Light")
Rodos - Lindos - Rodos: 5-6 times daily
Rodos - Afandou - Archangelos - Rodos: 10 times daily
Rodos - Kalithea - Rodos: 10 times daily
Rodos - Kalithie - Psinthos - Rodos: 3 times daily
Rodos - Massari - Rodos: 6 times daily
Rodos - Faliraki: 11 times daily
      Faliraki - Rodos: 5 times daily
Rodos - Laerma - Rodos: 1 time daily
Rodos - Kalathos - Rodos: 1 time daily
Rodos - Pylon - Rodos: 1 time daily
Rodos - Mesanaghros - Rodos: 1 time daily
Rodos - Apolakkia - Rodos: 1 time daily
Buses for the West Coast ("Nea Agora" - Averoff Str.)
Rodos - Koskinu - Rodos: 16 times daily, return 14 times daily
Rodos - Filerimos (Ialysos) - Rodos: Every half hour (via Trianda, Kremasti, Paradhision)
Rodos - Kalavardha - Rodos: 7 times daily, return 2 times daily
Rodos - Monolithos - Rodos: 1 time daily (via Salakos and Embonas)
Rodos - Kamiros - Rodos: 1 time daily (via Kamiros Skala, Kritinia, Embonas)
City Bus ("Nea Agora" - Averoff Str.)
No 3 Rodini Park: every half hour
No 4 Monte Smith (Aghios Ioannis): every half hour
For more information:
KTEL: 0241-20236 (for the island bus routes)
RODA: 0241-27462 (for the city transport)

CAMPING

There is only one camping site in Rhodos, near Lardhos. Officially, camping elsewhere on the island is prohibited. Check with N.T.O.G. for further information.

CAR RENTAL AND CAR-HIRE FIRMS

There are dozens of car hire firms in the city. The official prices are reasonable and negotiable most of the time. You can expect your car to be delivered at the airport or at your hotel.

Drivers should possess a national driving licence (EEC countries) or an international driving licence.

AJAX
5, Papalouka Str.
Tel: 0241-22508

ALFA
5, 28 Octovriou Str.
Tel: 0241-20253

AUTORENT
10, Ammohostou Str.
Tel: 0241- 25345, 25346

AVIS
9, Gallias Str.
Tel: 0241-24990, 23433
Rodos International Airport
Tel: 0241-92897

BUDGET RENT A CAR
– Ialysou Avenue
  Tel: 0241-22508
– Rodos International Airport
  Tel: 0241-93541

**CONDELLIS / AI-ANSA
INTERNATIONAL RENT A CAR**
45, Orfanidou Str.
Tel: 0241-22988

EURORENT RHODES
49, Papalouka Str.
Tel: 0241-28359, -33645
Tlx: 292-380

EUROPCAR
Ethelonton Dodecanision Str.
Tel: 0241-22816

HERTZ
10, Griva Str. (Grand Hotel)
Tel: 0241-21819, -25888
Tlx: 292-155

– 18, 28 Octovriou Str.
  Tel: 0241-21958, 32727
– Rodos International Airport
  Tel: 0241-93105

JUST RENT A CAR
45, Orfanidou Str.
Tel: 0241-31895, 22988

KOSTAS RENT A CAR
76, 28 Octovriou Str.
Tel.: 0241-25622

TOURENT
99, Sof. Venizelou Str.
Tel: 0241-25418, 21320

CAR SERVICE AND REPAIRS

Working Hours: Mon-Sat: 07.30-15.30
EMMANUEL NIKITAS 58, Strat. Zisi Str. Tel: 29371
KAKAKIOS TSAMBIKOS 48, Ialysos Ave. Tel: 91107

CASINO

A well known attraction of the island, housed in the Grand Hotel.
Games Available: American Roulette, Black Jack, Chemin de Fer, slot machines. Opening hours: 20.00-03.00, daily.

COMMUNICATIONS

Post Office:
Eleftherias Str. (Mandraki). Tel: 0241-22212
Working hours: Mon-Fri: 07.30-20.30
Telecommunication Centre (OTE)
130, Amerikis - 25 Martiou Str.
Working hours: Daily - 24 hours

CONSULATES

Austria: 8, G. Efstathiou Str. Tel: 0241-22393
Belgium: 15, Ir. Polytechniou Str. Tel: 0241-24180
Denmark: Ir. Polytechniou Str. Tel: 0241-25577
Ethiopia: 106, Kennedy Str. Tel: 0241-27642
Finland: Amerikis Str. D.A.N.E. Tel: 0241-20120
France: 31, Ag. Nikolaou Str. Tel: 0241-22318
Germany: 43, Kennedy Str. Tel: 0241-29730
Holland: 15, Ir. Polytechniou Str. Tel: 0241-24534
Italy: Ippoton Str. Tel: 0241-27342
Norway: 45, Orfanidou Str. Tel: 0241-22497
Sweden: 45, Makariou Str. Tel: 0241-21388
Spain: 11-13, Amerikis Str. Tel: 0241-22350
Turkey: 10, Ir. Polytechniou Str. Tel: 0241-23362
United Kingdom: 17, 25 Martiou Str. Tel: 0241-27306, 24963

CRIME and THEFT

Practically non-existent. In fact there is no jail in Rodos and law-breakers must be sent to Kos to be locked up.
In any case, if you lose something or suspect that it has been stolen from you, report it to your nearest Police Station or contact the Tourist Police immediately. They will be most helpful.

CURRENCY

The monetary unit of Greece is the drachma (abbreviated drs and δρχ in Greek). There are coins of 1, 2, 5, 10, 20 and 50 drachmas. Banknotes come in denominations of 50, 100, 500, 1,000 and 5,000 drachmas.

DRY CLEANING AND LAUNDERETTES

Working Hours: Mon-Fri: 08.00-22.00 Sat. 08.30-13.00
COLOSSOS 9, Othonos and Amalias Str. Tel: 29559
LAVOMATIC LAUNDERETTE 32, 28th Octovriou Str.
KRINOS 4, Eth. Dodekanision Str. Tel: 24917

ELECTRIC CURRENT

220-V, 50-cycle A.C.

EMERGENCIES

Fire Brigade	:	199
Police	:	100
Rodos Hospital	:	25555
ELPA	:	104
Tourist Police	:	27423

EXCHANGE

Foreign currency can be changed into drachmas at any local Bank during working hours (see also **BANKS**). There also is a Bureau of Change at Lindos. And, of course, you can pay in foreign currency in most of the hotels.

FESTIVALS

SOUND AND LIGHT SPECTACLE
Information: 0241-21922
Ticket price: 180 drs, students and pupils 70 drs.
Site: Municipal Gardens
Programme: Daily April 1 - October 31, except on full moon nights.

Apr. 1-May 15 & August 1-Oct. 31		May 16-July 31	
English	: 20.00 Mon, Tue	English	: 21.00 Mon, Tue
»	: 21.00 Wed, Fri, Sat	»	: 22.00 Wed, Fri, Sat
»	: 22.15 Thu	»	: 23.10 Thu
French	: 20.00 Wed, Sun	French	: 21.00 Wed, Sun
German	: 20.00 Fri, Sat	German	: 21.00 Fri, Sat
»	: 21.00 Tue, Thu	»	: 22.05 Tue, Thu
»	: 22.15 Wed	»	: 23.10 Wed
Swedish	: 20.00 Thu	Swedish	: 20.00 Sat
»	: 21.00 Mon	»	: 21.00 Thu
»	: 22.15 Tue, Sat	»	: 22.05 Mon
Greek	: 22.15 Sun	Greek	: 23.10 Tue

GREEK FOLK DANCES
by Nelly Dimoglou Group at Folk Dances Theatre-Old Town
May 1st - Oct. 31st
Ticket price: 700 drs, Students 500 drs.
Information: 0241-20157, 29085
Performances: Daily at 21.15, exc. Saturday

GUIDES

The official Guide Union of the Dodecanese islands has a skilled staff speaking English as well as other European languages.
Address: Makariou Str. Tel: 0241-27525

HAIRDRESSING

Working Hours: Hairdressers   Mon-Sat: 09.00-21.00
Sun and Holidays 09.00-13.00
Barbers   Mon-Fri: 08.00-21.00
Sat: 08.00-17.00
Sun and Holidays closed
ALFA 99, Amerikis Str. Tel: 23077
HAIR 83, D. Themeli Str. Tel: 23053
NIKOS 21, Iroon Polytechniou Str. Tel: 28704

HOSPITAL

Queen Olga Hospital
Hospital Hours: Out-patients 24 hours
Offices: 07.30-14.30
Operator: 0241-25 555

HYDROFOILS

s/s MARILENA, s/s TZINA Tel: 0241-24377
Rodos - Kos: 07.00 and 20.00 daily
Rodos - Patmos: 07.00 and 20.00 Tue, Thu, Sat
Rodos - Samos: 07.00 and 20.00 Fri
Rodos - Kalymnos - Leros: 07.00 and 20.00 Sun
Kos - Rodos: 08.00 and 21.00 daily

INFORMATION

National Tourist Organization of Greece (NTOG)
Makariou - Papagou Str. Tel: 0241-23255, 23655
Olympic Airways (O.A.) (See Airlines)
Tourist Police Tel: 0241-27423
Port Police Tel: 0241-27690, 22220
Automobile and Touring Club of Greece (ELPA) Operator: 104
Hotel Owners Association of Rhodes
8, Vas. Sofias Str. Tel: 0241-26446, Tlx: 292-150

KIOSKS

A number of unexpected items can be found in Greek Kiosks (called in Greek *"periptero"*). Apart from magazines, newspapers, cigarettes, post-cards, chocolates, you can also buy shoe-laces and polish, needles and thread, buttons etc. Open all day long, they are very useful when other shops are closed.

MOTORING

Entering Greece:
You'll need:
Either an International Driving Licence or your national driving licence
(EEC countries)

An international licence can be issued by the Automobile and Touring Club of Greece (ELPA), if you have an ordinary driving licence: Fee: 1,200 drs. Applicants are required to present:

a) Their passport or identity card, national driving licence and one photograph.
b) Car registration papers.
c) Nationality plate or sticker.
d) Green Card (not obligatory any more for citizens of EEC countries): an extension to your regular insurance policy, making it valid for foreign countries.

Driving Regulations:

Road signs and traffic regulations are in line with international standards. Traffic travels on the right, with overtaking on the left. Wearing seatbelts is now obligatory. It is an offence to drive after drinking *any* alcohol. Motorcycle and motorscooter drivers - as well as passengers - must wear helmets. The speed limit for passenger vehicles is 50 km/h in built-up areas, 80 km/h on country roads and 100 km/h on motor ways and expressways.

Driving Conditions:

All roads in and around the city of Rodos are in a good condition, becoming progressively worse as you head towards the southern part of the island. Traffic to and from the villages during summertime is usually heavy.

Fuel and Oil:

Service and gas stations are plentiful on the island, but be careful since they close at 19.00. One, in each area, though, stays open till midnight. To spot which one call-free of charge - the Automobile and Touring Club of Greece (tel: 104) or find it in a local newspaper.

MUSEUMS

ACROPOLIS - THEATRE - STADIUM Tel: 0241-27674
Open: Daily 09.00-15.30, Sundays & Holidays 10.00-15.00
Admission free.
MUSEUM Tel: 0241-27674
Open: Daily 08.00-19.00, Sundays & Holidays 09.00-19.00
Closed on Tuesdays. Entrance fee: Drs. 150.
PALACE OF THE KNIGHTS Tel: 0241-27674
Open: Daily 08.00-19.00, Sundays & Holidays 09.00-19.00
Closed on Tuesdays. Entrance fee: Drs. 150.
PERIMETRE OF THE MEDIEVAL WALLS Tel: 0241-27674
Open to visitors accompanied by a guide on Monday and Saturday afternoons. Visitors should gather in the courtyard of the Palace of the Knights.
Open: Daily 16.00-19.00
Admission free.
CAMIROS EXCAVATIONS Tel: 0241-27674
Open: Daily 08.00-19.00, Sundays & Holidays 09.00-19.00
Entrance fee: Drs. 100.
ACROPOLIS OF IALYSOS Tel: 0241-27674
Open: Daily 09.00-15.30, Sundays & Holidays 10.00-15.00
Entrance fee: Drs. 100.
ACROPOLIS OF LINDOS Tel: 0241-27674
Open: Daily 08.00-19.00, Sundays & Holidays 09.00-19.00
Entrance fee: Drs. 150.
DECORATIVE COLLECTIONS Tel: 0241-27674
It is open to the public on Mondays, Wednesdays and Fridays from 09.00-13.00. Entrance fee: Drs. 100.

NEWSPAPERS and MAGAZINES

Most of Europe's and USA's big daily newspapers can be found in Rodos in kiosks, tourist shops and big hotels' news-stands. The same applies to magazines as well as weeklies. Please note that the foreign dailies arrive one

TRADITIONAL DANCE CENTER
GREEK FOLK DANCES
By NELLY DIMOGLOU

OLD TOWN THEATRE
ANDRONIKOU and ANTIOTHIOU

Every night at 21.15 ,
except Saturday,
from May to October.

The civilization of yesterday
in the life of today.
Become acquainted
with Greece, through
Greek folk tradition.
Dances and songs
in local costumes.

A night you must not miss.

Information:

RHODES
93, Venetokleous Str.
Tel. (0241) 20157, 29085

ATHENS
89, Dekelias Str.
Nea Philadelphia
Tel. (01) 2510801

day late. For brief news you can pick up "Athens News" or "Athens Star", the Greek daily papers in English.

PHARMACIES

Working Hours: Mon, Wed, Sat: 08.00-14.00
Tue, Thu, Fri: 08.00-13.00 16.00-20.00
Note that there is one pharmacy stand-by for emergencies every day from 13.00 till next morning. For name and address check with the nearest pharmacy. There will be a notice on its windowcase.

POLICE

Emergency Squad   : 100
Tourist Police   : 27423
Rodos Airport Station : 92881
Rodos Port Police   : 27690, 22220

PUBLIC HOLIDAYS and FEAST DAYS

In addition to the official Greek public Holidays (with banks, offices and shops closed) which are celebrated all over the island, there are some more holidays of local interest.

Public Holidays

Jan. 1	New Year's Day
Jan. 6	Epiphany Day
March	Shrove Monday (Movable Date)
March 25	Greek Independence Day
April/May	Good Friday (Movable Date)
April/May	Easter Monday (Movable Date)
May 1	May Day
Aug. 15	Assumption Day
Oct. 28	Ochi ("No") Day
Dec. 25	Christmas Day
Dec. 26	St. Stephen's Day

Holidays of local interest:

Apr. 23	Aghios Georgios in Kritinia
Jun. 15	Aghios Amos in Faliraki
Jun. 29	Aghioi Petros and Pavlos in Lindos
Jul. 17	Aghia Marina in Asguru, Koskinu and Paradision
Jul. 20	Profitis Ilias in the Profitis Ilias Monastery
Jul. 27	Aghios Pandeleimon in Sianna
Aug. 6	Metamorphosis in Maritsa
Aug. 15	Kimissis tis Theotokou (Assumption of the Mother of God) especially in Embonas and Kremasti
Sept. 8	Genissis tis Theotokou (Nativity of the Mother of God) in the Tsambika Monastery
Sept. 14	Timios Stavros in Kalithea
Sept. 26	Aghios Ioannis Theologos in Artamita Monastery
Oct. 18	Aghios Loukas in Afandou
Nov. 8	Michail Archangelos in Symi island

ORGANIZED TOURS

From Athens
RODOS BY AIR-TWO DAYS
Organizers: Got, Key
CRETE - RODOS BY AIR-THREE DAYS
Organizers: Got, Key
RODOS - CRETE BY AIR - FOUR DAYS
Organizers: Chat

RADIO and TV

There are three programmes on the Greek Radio and two TV channels. On both these media there are news bulletins in English at certain hours of the day. Your hotel desk or "Athens News" can provide you with a broadcast schedule.

RELIGIOUS SERVICES

Catholic. At St. Mary's Catholic church mass is said in Latin on weekdays at 19.00 and on Sundays at 08.00 and 11.00 and 19.00. In the summertime part of the mass may be in English.

Protestant. Inquire at St. Mary's church since visiting clergymen sometimes conduct Protestant Services there during the tourist season.

Jewish. The 17th - century Sholom Synagogue, (Dosiadou Str.) is open for prayer.

RESTAURANTS AND NIGHT LIFE

Eating Out and Restaurants

With a centuries-long tradition of catering for visitors, and now attracting holidaymakers from all over the world, Rodos offers food and entertainment round the clock.

Breakfast is served early or late, bars and cafés offer a wide choice of coffees and drinks when you want them - and the way you like them. Enjoy Greek ouzo or raki with *"mezes"* (a little something to eat is always served with ouzo), Scotch whisky, Irish coffee, American cocktails. Try Rodos' own cocktail, Lumumba, a mix of chocolate milk and brandy, a completely new experience and a perfect accompanyment to Greek sweetmeats laden with chopped nuts and honey.

Dining out under the stars is one of the most enjoyable experiences of a Greek holiday and Rodos is particularly well supplied with restaurants and tavernas offering the holidaymaker a genuine local atmosphere. Town and countryside each have their attractions. Every beauty spot has its own charm and just off the main road to Lindos, there is a restaurant perched on the rocks in the middle of a stream.

The island cuisine caters for all tastes and internationally known dishes are available in most restaurants. The Scandinavians will find their smorgesbord, the French their snails (a traditional delicacy in Greece, too), and the English their roast beef. Those who stick to the known dishes, though, will never know the real taste of the Mediterranean.

Beef, pork, lamb and goat's meat or fish taste good whether roasted over softly glowing charcoals or oven-cooked in the delicious sauces in which they are served. The sauces are most usually based on tomato, with water, olive oil and herbs added. Vegetables, too, are often cooked this way in deli-

A wine... 2300 years old.

Gold-plated wine crater, found 2300 years ago in Macedonia, near the TSANTALI winery which reveals the great tradition of the Macedonians in the art of good wine-making.

Makedoniko Tsantali

Centuries ago, the Macedonians established the tradition that entails numerous secrets, passed from generation to generation. Today, still following the same, 2300 years old tradition, we are making the MAKEDONIKO TSANTALI. This tradition, together with the TSANTALIS' craftsmanship, endows the MAKEDONIKO with the rich aroma and the distinctive taste of fresh grapes. Just uncork and enjoy the MAKEDONIKO TSANTALI. White or rosé, in a green bottle.

TSANTALI 🍇 WINE
greek sunshine

TAVERNE Alexis

since 1957

sea food

18, Socratous Str. Old Town Tel.: 29347

cious combinations. Of course, every cook has a favourite recipe handed down from generation to generation of hearty eaters.

In a taverna the food is usually on view for diners to choose what appeals to the eye - an opportunity for you to find out what those mysterious menu items really are. In larger establishments the menu will be written in English as well as in Greek.

Before the main dish is served order *"mezes"* - this time slightly different to those in the *"ouzeri"*. In smallish portions and served to the table, everyone takes a little of what they fancy. This is an excellent way to try something new. A dish of creamy *"tzatziki"* (yoghurt with shredded cucumber and garlic), salmon coloured *"taramosalata"* (a dip made with a base of fish roe and creamed potatoes, beaten smooth), *"melitsanosalata"* or *"melitsanes tiganites"* (aubergine creamed or sliced and fried), *"humus"* (chick pea spread), or *"gigantes"* (giant white beans cooked in sauce). Other include *"dolmades"* (stuffed vine leaves); *"keftedes"* (small meat balls flavoured with mint and oregano, an unusual combination to tease the palate); *"mousaka"* (alternate layers of sliced aubergine, minced beef and tomato sauce, covered with bechamel sauce and baked with a topping of grated cheese); stuffed zucchini, tomatoes or peppers; fried cheese and many others, both traditional and specialities of the house.

You will find yourself left with plenty of time to enjoy these before the dishes arrive. This is not due to lack of interest on the part of the proprietor - it is traditional in Greece to relax and converse over a leisurely evening meal. As you are on holiday you can do the same.

Follow your meal with fresh fruit in season. Melons, watermelons, apricots, peaches, figs and grapes all taste better when freshly gathered.

Choosing a wine to drink with your meal will not be any problem. There are wines from all over Greece, and other countries too. But Rodians have been making wine since time immemorial and have a good range to choose from, including the white "Ilios" and "Grand Maitre" and famous dry red "Chevalier de Rhodes", while Rodian champagnes are themselves cause for celebration.

Lunch is usually served from 12.00 to 15.00, dinner from 20.00 to midnight Most of the restaurants though, stay open till 03.00.

Here is a list of some of the restaurants and tavernas of the city, where you can have a proper meal.

PIZZERIAS:
COLOSSOS 28, Ammohostou Str. Tel: 27981
LA PIZZAGIO 60, Kanada Str. Tel: 25581
MON AMI 23, I. Dragoumi Str.
NAPOLEON 1, Othonos & Amalias Str. Tel: 26185
OLYMPIA PIZZA 12, 25th Martiou Str. Tel: 21620
PIZZERIA DEL VESUVIO 92, Griva Str. Tel: 27819
RESTAURANTS AND TAVERNAS
AGOSTINO 582, Apostolou Pavlou Str. Tel: 31218
ALEXIS (sea food) 18, Socratous Str. Tel: 29347, 26717
ARGO (sea food) 23-24, Hippocratous Sq. Tel: 34232
CAPTAIN'S HOUSE 5, A. Zervou Str. Tel: 26836
CORAL 10, Iroon Politechniou Str. Tel: 20210
CYPRUS TAVERNA - MANDI'S PLACE 20 Shops Area. Tel: 32574
DANISH HOUSE 22, Akti Miaouli, Orfanidou Str. Tel: 20053
DELUKAS 19, Kos Str. Tel: 27680
ELLINIKON 29, Alex. Diakou Str. Tel: 28111
GEORGES G. Leondos Str. Tel: 20898
KON-TIKI Mandraki. Tel: 22477
LA BELLE EPOQUE Amerikis and 25th Martiou Str. Tel: 26406
LA MAISON FLEURIE Riga Fereou Str. Tel: 25340
MYKONOS 31, V. Constantinou Str. Tel: 27287
MYLOS 204, M.Petridis Str. Tel: 33150
NOBEL 19, Griva Str. Tel: 26066
OSCAR 4, Iroon Polytechniou Str. Tel: 23247
PANORAMA Kalithea Ave. (to Koskinou). Tel: 82426
PAPAGALO Akti Miaouli & Mandilara Str.
PLAKA (sea food) Ippocratous Sq. Old Town
ROMA 62, Sof. Venizelou Str. Tel: 29712
SCANDIA 12, Iroon Polytechniou Str. Tel: 28665

SIERRA EL PAELLA 1, Tilou Str. Tel: 21356
SOFIA 28, Orfeos Str. - Old Town Tel: 22674
VLACHOS 22, Them. Sofouli Str. Tel: 32287

ENTERTAINMENT AND NIGHT LIFE

Entertainment is taken seriously in Rodos and there is something for all. The ancient tragedies and comedies are played at the Old Stadium, the Sound and Light Show can be visited in the evening, and the Nelly Dimoglou group gives nightly performances of traditional dances from all parts of Greece. There is traditional and modern music and songs in the tavernas and nightclubs and everyone should have a go at trying the steps of such dances as the "syrtaki" where hands are joined and everyone follows the leader. The solo "zeibekikos" should not be interrupted, since it is a spontaneous expression of the spirit of the dancer, happy or sad.

In the Old Town, tavernas lie hidden in palm-lined courtyards, where musicians play romantic music for dining and dancing under a roof of vines and swaying palm trees. There is often a favourite dish which is worth trying; ask the waiter to help you choose.

Clustered around Mandraki Harbour and in the narrow streets of the Old Town fish restaurants serve grilled octopus, crisp fried baby squid, big pale pink shrimps and small Mediterranean lobsters. If you have never tasted swordfish you have a treat to come. This is a noisy cheerful place, the music is lively and discos abound. Dance on the sea in the lively and crowded floating restaurant.

Over on Akti Miaouli the Casino in the Grand Hotel Astir Palace lures the rich, the reckless and the merely bored, who seek the spice of uncertainty.

Spun out along the coast road are restaurants, tavernas, night clubs, and discos offering good food, wine, music and song. From Rodos to Ialysos the road is lined with luxurious hotels, night clubs, "bouzoukia" and discos. As the sun sets over the Mediterranean and the lights spring up, half the world seems to be here. Top class musicians and internationally known cabaret stars are there to amuse you. Entertainment is available in a big way, and you can join in an exciting throng where the holidaymaker is king.

Here is a list of some renowned night-spots.

CAFETERIAS, BARS AND PUBS
AKTAEON CAFE Mandraki Harbour
CAFE ROYAL 8-10, Al. Diakou Str. Tel: 20122
CARMEN PUB 65, Al. Diakou Str. Tel: 30357
IALYSSOS 8, Ierou Lohou Str. Ialysos. Tel: 92431
JOHNNY'S PUB 8, Iroon Politechniou Str. Tel: 22576
LA LUNA PUB 6th Km Kalithea Ave. Tel: 82498
MIKE'S 17, Voriou Ipirou Str.
PARFAIT 54, G. Lambraki Str. Tel: 28540
PUB ZOOM 1, Kos Str. Tel: 27783
SALOON 13, Iroon Politechniou Str.
TIVOLI 51, Griva Str. Tel: 32766
TRIANON Academy Sq. Tel: 22838
WHITE ROCK PUB 22B, Amalias - Othonos Str. Tel: 30639

DISCOS
BERMUDA 13, Iroon Polytechniou Str. Tel: 32035
HIWAY 105, Ialysos Ave. Tel: 33660
JOHN PLAYER'S SPECIAL Academy Sq. Tel: 32844
MORE 18, Sof. Venizelou Str. Tel: 20358
PLAYBOY DISCO CLUB, (opposite Hotel Miramare). Tel: 28815
SPACE 14, Iroon Polytechniou Str. Tel: 30380

NIGHT CLUBS AND GREEK MUSIC
BLUE BIRD Night Club (BLUE SKY Hotel). Tel: 24091
BLUE NOTE Night Club 30, Al. Diakou Str. Tel: 34582
CAFE CHANTANT Greek Music 22, Aristotelous Str. Old Town. Tel: 32277
COPACABANA Night Club. Tel: 21744, 20251
COSMPOLITAN Night Club.Tel: 26800
LA CITE 32, Akti Miaouli. Tel: 21946
RETRO 12, Riga Fereou Str. Tel: 25163
RODOS BY NIGHT Night Club (Opposite Hotel Miramare). Tel: 28675
ZORBAS Greek Music 4, Iroon Polytechniou Str.

Night Club
BLUE BIRD

BLUE SKY HOTEL - RODOS
TEL.: 24-091

*Live Rock
and Disco Music
International Program*

The most famous Night Club in Rodos, where
you can dance till morning, listening to the last
Rock and Disco music hits from our orchestra.
You can also enjoy youself
listening to the Greek program, where we
proudly present the world known
bouzouki player GRIGORIS TSISTOUDIS.

Every night lots of fun and dancing.

SHOPPING

Taking a stroll through the ultra-modern shopping area of the new town or exploring the cobbled streets of the medieval walled city, the Old Town, shopping in Rodos is a unique opportunity. In 1947, when the Dodecanese islands were finally reunited with Greece they were granted a special duty-free status which they enjoy to this day. Even allowing for the cost of transport for imported goods, this makes for good shopping and it is possible to buy many quality products at prices lower than in the country where they are made. Scotch whisky, from all the better known distilleries, can be bought for less than anywhere else in the world.

Without a cloud in the sky the ubiquitous umbrella displays seem to indicate an expectation of sudden storms. Not so, the umbrellas are just another duty-free item ever popular with shoppers. Of course, like everywhere else, prices vary and it is sensible to shop around for the best value.

Top quality British fabrics, Harris tweeds, worsteds and cashmere, are sold here and custom-made suits and dresses can be produced by the island's expert tailors in a few days. Garments and sports wear by world - famous names are available at prices which would tempt the most cautious shopper to overspend. Naturally, American Express, Access, Diners, and other Credit cards are accepted everywhere.

Of course not everything is imported. Rodos has a constant influx of visitors looking for quality goods and many beautiful things are made on the island. Furs are among some of the best buys anywhere in Greece and Rodos is no exception. The finest minks can be bought at a very good saving, and for those with shallower pockets remarkably beautiful coats and jackets can be found at unbelievable prices. The secret is that these latter are made up from tiny scraps that would otherwise be wasted. Again, furs can be made to measure, but take a little longer than fabric garments to make.

Fashionable shoes are made here and the high quality models which are made for export are an excellent buy.

In Greece the production of jewellery is not a production line operation, but is still in the hands of families of proud craftsmen whose skilled fingers have wrought fine designs to new themes and old ones for many generations. From copies of jewellery made by the craftsmen of old to the most modern designs of the present-day goldsmith or silversmith, there is an infinite variety of exquisite trinkets from which to choose, and the reflection of the sun on countless gold chains, rings, necklaces, earrings and pendants dazzles the eye. These are ideal purchases for someone looking for something uniquely Greek. The elaborate silver filligree jewellery of Rodos, set with semi precious stones, is known throughout Europe and the Middle East.

Pottery jars were another ancient export from Rodos, usually full of wine - the most popular items today are plates from Lindos with brightly painted floral patterns, ships or fish.

Many other traditional craft items which are still popular today can be found in the Turkish bazaar round in the Old Town and this is a fascinating place to shop. Leather bags and purses, brass and copper wares, worry beads in all sizes and materials, costume dolls, woven spreads, rugs and bags, shirts and dresses are among the thousands of items that can be found in these small treasure houses. Bargain! Prices are not usually considered fixed and a little haggling is part of the pleasure of the transaction for both buyer and seller. Better prices can always be obtained by buying several things together in one shop.

SHOPPING HOURS
General Trade Stores: Mon-Fri 08.00-13.00 and 17.00-21.00
                        Sat 08.00-14.00
Super Markets: Mon-Fri 07.00-13.00 and 17.00-21.00
                  Sat 07.00-15.00
Tourist Shops: (Greek handicrafts, jewellery, leather goods etc.)
                Mon-Sat 08.00-22.00
                Sun and Holidays 10.00-22.00

The list contains only some of the shops of the lot that can be found in Rodos.

CHILDREN'S WEAR
ASTERIX 25, Tarpon Springs Str. Tel: 26832
BABY CLUB 43, Theodoraki Str. Tel: 21370
BOUBOU JOLIE 27, Eth. Dodekanision Str. Tel: 31191

BOOKS - STATIONERY
HADZIIOANNOU 29, Tarpon Springs Str. Tel: 24219
MAKRIS & SON 10, Plastira Str. Tel: 24215
TOMARAS 5-7, Venizelou Str. Tel: 32055
TSELIOS 6, Ethel. Dodekanision Str. Tel: 25969

COSMETICS AND PERFUMES
BEAUTY-A. CHARALAMBIDES 18-19 Nea Agora Str. Tel: 27429
PAPAGAPITOS & SON 11, Ethn. Makariou Str. Tel: 24247

DEPARTMENT STORES
PAPPOU 7, 25th Martiou Str. Tel: 24286
STOP AND SHOP 26, 28th Octovriou Str. Tel: 27458
TANAGRA 5B, Ionos Dragoumi Str. Tel: 22021
THE ROSE 9, Vas. Constantinou Str.

FASHION AND SPORTSWEAR
AMICA BOUTIQUE 5, Amerikis Str. Tel: 28788
CARRERA 5, Gallias Str. Tel: 25925
ELLESSE Gallias Str. New Market. Tel: 24779
HADZIMANOLIS 12, Gallias Str. Tel: 27779
KARAYIANNIS 1, 25th Martiou Str. Tel: 29502
LAGOSTINO 20, Othonos-Amalias Str. Tel: 21742
LE CROCODILE 39, Amerikis Str. Tel: 21253
NAFSIKA BOUTIQUE 27, Theodoraki Str. Tel: 35947
PAPAPANAYIOTIS BOUTIQUE 48, Lambraki Str. Tel: 21786
PATRICIA BOUTIQUE Academy Sq.
RODEO 35, G. Lambraki Str. Tel: 25656
ROUBETI BOUTIQUE 30, Iroon Polytechniou Str. Tel: 20616
SCARABEE 11, Cyprus Sq. Tel: 22710, 35400
VALSAMI 24, Gallias Str. Tel: 24323, 24259

FISHING EQUIPMENT
PANAGOS-SPANOS 5, Al. Papagou Str. Tel: 27765

FLORISTS
BAKALOUMAS 81, Annas Marias Str. Tel: 23951
BLOEMENLAND 32, Grigoriou E. Str. Tel: 25913
NARKISSOS 64, Sof. Venizelou Str. Tel: 20980
ORFANOS-LOIZOS 24, G. Leondos Str. Tel: 24216
THEMELI P. Germanou - Ag. Anastasias Str. Tel: 23951

FURS
ANAGNOSTOU FURS 17, Vas. Constantinou Str. Tel: 24158
DIMITRIS CREATIONS 2, Othonos and Amalias Str. Tel: 21317
INTERFURS 27-30, Ippocratous Sq. Tel: 29802
MARIOS 72-74, Socratous Str. Tel: 25544, 24900
PERIDIS 18, Vas. Constandinou Str. Tel: 22886
SMART FURS 4, Griva Str. Tel: 20747
STUDIO EXCLUSIVE FURS 64, Socratous Str. Tel: 23752

furs
ANAGNOSTOU

17, VASSILEOS CONSTANTINOU Str. TEL.: 24-158
OPPOSITE "HOTEL DES ROSES" (CORNER)
EXPOSITION AND FACTORY TEL.: 24-959, 22-737

GIFTS
CHRISTOFLE 8, Amerikis and Ierou Lohou Str. Tel: 27127
EPSILON HELLAS 5, Gallias Str. Tel: 34288
MIKE 65, Ermou Str. Tel: 32915
NOVELTEX 10, Griva Str. Tel: 28439
RODIN 1, Iroon Politechniou Str. Tel: 31144
TRIK MAI FORT 14, Al. Diakou Str. Tel: 35960
THEODOSIA 11, Vas. Constantinou Str. (opposite Hotel Rodon).
VALLEY OF THE BUTTERFLY 28, Eth. Dodecanision Str. Tel: 25232

JEWELLERY
CHRIS GOLD 177, Socratous Str. Old Town. Tel: 20915
M. MENTOS 33, Apellou Str. Tel: 23935
TZIVELEK 1, Socratous Str. Tel: 21049
ZOLOTAS 34, E. Makariou Str. Tel: 23001

LEATHER GOODS
ALAVANOS SAVAS 23, Othonos and Amalias Str. Tel: 31983
M.G. FASHION IN LEATHER 46, G. Lambraki Str. Tel: 21566
MOCASSINO 25th Martiou & Dodekanision Str. Tel: 28156
VENDETTA Averof and Karpathou Str. Tel: 26817
ZERVOS 30, Griva Str. (New Town). Tel: 25260
        32, Lahitos Str. (Old Town). Tel: 25143

PHOTOGRAPHY AND FILMS
PHOTO-ECONOMOU 169, Socratous Str. Tel: 22043
PHOTO-EXPRESS 54, Gr. Lambraki Str. Tel: 28540
PHOTO-EXPRESS LAPPAS 27, Othonos and Amalias Str. Tel: 30243
SAKELARIDIS & Co. 4-6, Ethn. Makariou Str. Tel: 27361
SPEEDY'S PHOTO SERVICE 40, Karpathou Str. Tel: 24744

POTTERY AND CERAMICS
BABIS CERAMICS 7th Km Kalithea Ave. Tel: 27288, 82477
NASOS CERAMICS 8, Menekleous Str. Old Town
NINA 32, Griva Str. Tel: 25917
VOYAZIS & SON 2, Ammochostou Str. Tel: 25516

RECORD SHOPS
HI-FI 20, Gr. Lambraki Str. Tel: 21282
SOUND Academy Sq. Tel: 26281
TOP TEN 57, Sof. Venizelou Str. Tel: 21283

SHOES
CAVADAS & SON 34, Amerikis Str. Tel: 25150
MOSHOUTIS 5, Iroon Polytechniou Str. Tel: 25839
PETRIDIS (men's, ladies') Vas. Constantinou & Gr. Digeni Str., Tel: 25936
SEVASTAKIS (ladies') 32, Alex. Diakou Str. Tel: 23541
24, (men's, ladies', children's) 39, Eth. Makariou Str. Tel: 27978

TEXTILES
ASPRAKIS 33, Ethn. Makariou Str. Tel: 20247
EUROPEAN-FERTAKIS 33, Tarpon Springs Str. Tel: 30252
HADZISTAVRIDIS 31, Gr. Lambraki Str. Tel: 28294
KATSARAS 7, Ethn. Makariou Str. Tel: 27314
VAKONDIOS 89, 25th Martiou Str. Tel: 29500

Tzivelek

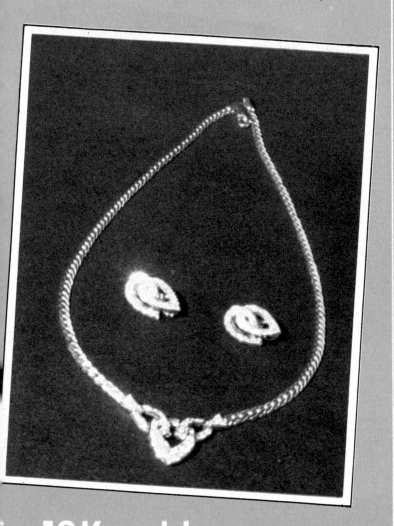

INTERNATIONAL
MINI GOLF

J. FINAS
INTERNATIONAL
MINI - GOLF
18 Holes

2, Kastelorizou Str. (near 100 Palmiers) RHODES

SPORTS

Golf: There is a golf course at Xenia Hotel Afandou, 19km south from the city of Rodos. Golf course with: 18 holes. 6.135 m for men, PAR 73, 5,540 m for women. Tel: 0241-51225-6-7, 51541.

Tennis: Many of the island hotels have courts, some of which are open to the public, with tennis equipment available to be hired on the spot. Ask your hotel desk-clerk for information. The Rodos Athletic Centre with its own courts can help you too.

Sailing: You can get information on the chartering of small sailing boats or participating in regattas from: Rodos Yachting Club 9, Koundouriotou Square, Tel: 0241-23287.

Skin-diving: You can do it but bear in mind that tampering or removing any archaeological remains that you may find on the seabed is strictly forbidden. In fact, you're expected to report any such finding to the authorities.

Spear fishing: Very popular. It is forbidden to go spear fishing with scuba equipment, and you won't be allowed within 100 meters from the public beaches.

Waterskiing, paraskiing: The eastern coast is more suitable since wind and sea are calmer. You can hire all the suitable equipment in some of the hotels and on Faliraki and Lindos Beaches.

Wind-surfing: The most popular sport. If you don't have your own equipment you can always hire it on the beaches of the big hotels.

Hunting: A licence is required. For information and help contact Rodia Elafos Club in town. The hunting season runs from August 25 to March 10 for most game. August 25 to September 30 for migratory birds. November 1 to January 10 for rabbits and partridge.

Fishing: The best fishing grounds are off the shores of Lindos, Kamiros, Kallithea and Gennadi.

TAXIS

Taxis in Rodos are dark blue and bear the sign "TAXI" on the roof. You can get one of them anywhere in the city. All of them have meters.

Central Terminal: Rimini Square, Mandraki, tel: 27666.

Minimum Charge: 110 drs.

Tariffs: Single within the city limits. Double tariff begins from the Poseidon Hotel and from the Cemetery outwards. Also during the hours 01.00-05.00.

Hiring a taxi: You can hire a taxi for a few hours, a day or more. Prices are subject to negotiation.

Tips: Tipping is not actually expected, but a rounding up of the fare is.

CHARTER A VALEF YACHT

SINCE 1969 owners and managers of the largest fleet of crewed yachts for charter in Greece

FOR LESS THAN THE COST OF A HOTEL ROOM

IN GREECE

M/Y Christina, 160´, 7 staterooms, 6 similar yachts available.

M/Y Alexandra, 72´, 4 staterooms, 20 similar yachts available.

M/S Prince de Neufchatel, 85´, 30 similar yachts available.

For less than the price of checking into a hotel room, you can check out the thousands of hidden islands, the tucked-away beaches and the quaint fishing villages of the Greek Isles in your own, fully crewed, luxury yacht. Snorkel in a secluded cove, water ski from your yacht's private ski boat, explore the remains of an ancient civilization or just relax whenever or wherever you choose to cruise. If it sounds like a vacation fit for a millionaire, it is.

Except that this dream holiday costs no more per day than an average hotel room. In fact, it may even cost less! So find out for yourself why it pays to charter a Valef Yacht and leave the crowds, the pollution, the lines and everyday hustle. Turn a hotel room key and you open the door to four walls. Charter a Valef Yacht and you open the door to an Aegean adventure you'll never forget. Please write/phone for our brochure.

 VALEF YACHTS LTD

USA HEADQUARTERS: 7254 Fir Rd., AMBLER, PA 19002 U.S.A., Tel.: (215) 641.1624 or (215) 641.0423 or (1800) 223.3845
Telex: 846146 VAL AMBR
INTL. HEADQUARTERS: 22, AKTI THEMISTOKLEOUS, 185 36 PIRAEUS, GREECE, Tel.: 4529571, EVENINGS: 4529.486
Telex: 21-2000 VAL GR

TIME

Greece is in the East European Time Zone, 2 hours ahead of Greenwich Mean Time.

TIPPING:

In Greece, by law, all service charges are included in the bill at hotels, restaurants, bars etc. You can notice that on menus two prices are always quoted (one without and one with the service charges). Even though Greeks are not tip-crazy they usually expect you to leave an extra tip, both for the waiter and/or his assistant. It is a sensible thing to do, especially if you intend to visit that particular place again.

TRAVEL AGENCIES

AEGEAN TOURS Ltd.
7-9, G. Efstathiou Str. P.O. Box 189
Tel 29990-3, 24080, Tlx 292-113, Cbl Egeomar

AIRTOUR HELLAS
4-6, Kastelorizou Str. Tel 25160, 25142, Tlx 292-138

APOLLON TRAVEL
32, Al. Diakou Str. P.O. Box 306, Tel 28440, 28443,
Tlx 292-146

ARGO Ltd.
28-30, Iroon Polytechniou Str. Tel 24927, 20681,
Tlx 292-124

BAKARIS TRAVEL
7, Al. Diakou Str. P.O. Box 100, Tel 26231, 31525, 31531
Tlx 292-240

CACTUS TRAVEL
3, Amerikis Str. Tel 31225, 32383, Tlx 292-411

CARAYANIDES TRAVEL SERVICE S.A.
30, Iroon Polytechniou Str.
tel 24382, 22602, Tlx 292-130 Cbl Carigan

COLOSSUS TOURS & TRAVEL AGENCY
1, New Market Str. Tel 20852, 27463
Member of: IATA (code 27-2 8281

ELAFOS TRAVEL Ltd.
17e, Vass. Konstantinou Str. Tel 27766, 23066, 20466,
Tlx 292-105

ERETA TOURS
11, Kazouli Str. Tel 21571-2, 20532, Tlx 292-142

GEORGIADIS Ltd. TOURISM-SHIPPING
41, Vassilissis Sophias Avenue, Tel 27493, Cbl Frage

GOLDEN SUN HOLIDAYS Ltd. TRAVEL & TOURISM
20, M. Petridi Str. Tel 24592, 30644, Tlx 292-342
Member of: HATTA

GREECE INTER TRAVEL AGENCY
40, Amerikis Str. Tel 25545, Tlx 292-198

GREEK AIR HOLIDAYS Ltd.
1a, 25 Martiou Str. Tel 26977, 25511, Tlx 292-228

GREEK STAR Ltd.
21, Kathopouli Str. P.O. Box 232
Tel 24986, 23664, 21340, Tlx 292-149, Cbl Greekstar

HELIOS TOURS
32, 28 Octovriou Str.
Tel 24734, 22387, Tlx 292-118, Cbl Heliotour

HELLAS TRAVEL & TOURIST ENTERPRISES Ltd.
2, Sof. Venizelou Str. P.O. Box 30
Tel 23350, 27698, Tlx 292-133, Cbl Naftellas
Member of: IATA (code 27-2 1889)

HELLENIC TOURS
29, 25th Martiou Str. P.O. Box 25
Tel 21366, 20782, Cbl Melarod
Member of: IATA (code 27-2 0042)

IALYSSOS TRAVEL
27, Alex. Diakou Str. P.O. Box 149, Tel 31571 (4 lines),
Tlx 292-225

IBISCUS TOURS
1, Cyprus Square, Tel 27313, 27756, Tlx 292-136

INTERNATIONAL TRAVEL SERVICE
83, D. Themeli Str. Tel 24404, 28036, Tlx 292-257

INTEUROPA TOURS Ltd.
4-6, Kastellorizou Str. Tel 25142, Tlx 292-138

KASTRO TRAVEL
49, Amerikis Str. Tel 21008, Tlx 292-386
Member of: IATA (code 27-2 0043)

KAVADAS TRAVEL & TOURIST AGENCY
20, Karpathou Str. Tel 22156, 24940
Member of: IATA (code 27-2 1551)

KOUROS TRAVEL& TOURIST AGENCY
16, Gallias Str. Tel 22400, 24377, 24340, Tlx 292-141
Member of: IATA (code 27-2 8031), ASTA, FUAAV

KRONOS
30b, Cyprus Square, Tel 24428, 24000

KYDON TOURIST & SHIPPING AGENCY
14, Ethelondon Dodekanission Str. P.O. Box 49
Tel 23000, 27900, 27417, 32741, Tlx 292-347
Member of: IATA (code 27-2 0073)

MANOUSSOS TRAVEL
9, Akti Kanari, Tel 23231, 23137, 23531, 20167, Tlx 292-104

MOSCHATOS TRAVEL & TOURIST BUREAU
16, Karpathos Str. P.O. Box 216, Tel 23078, 22866, Tlx 292-139
Member of: HATTA

PALLAS TRAVEL
Lindos Village, 853 00 Rodos
Tel (0244) 31275, 31396, Tlx 292-502, Cbl Pallastour

PANDAIR Ltd.
42-48, Amerikis Str. Tel 28959. Tlx 292-254

PANORAMA TRAVEL
54, Alex. Diakou Street, P.O. Box 57
Tel 21130, 21133, 20131, 20132, 20152, 34097, Tlx 292-166

PLOTIN OF RHODES S.A.
23-25, 28th Octovriou Str. P.O. Box 237
Tel 20691 (4 lines), Tlx 292-147, 292-101

RED SEA TRAVEL TRADE & SHIPPING AGENCY
11-13, Amerikis Str. P.O. Box 158
Tel 22683, 22460, 27721, Tlx 292-158, Cbl Pak

PHODIAN VILLAGE HOLIDAYS
49, Papalouka Str. Tel 28359, 33645, Tlx 292-380

RHODES UNLIMITED
46, Vas. Sophias Str. Tel 28487, 29697, 29698, Tlx 292-249

RHODOS TOURS Ltd.
23, Amochostou Str. Tel 21010-13, Tlx 292-156

RINGAS TRAVEL & TOURISM BUREAU
15, Vas. Konstantinou Str. Tel 22960, 23060, Tlx 292-148

RODINI TOURS
13, Alexandrou Diakou Str. Tel 21535, 21562, 31355,
Tlx 292-350

RODOS EXPRESS TRAVEL SERVICE
Vas. Konstantinou & Amerikis Str. P.O. Box 353
Tel 21303 (3 lines), Tlx 292-271, 292-272
Member of: HATTA

RODOS ORION TOURS Ltd.
29, Eth. Dodekanission Str. Tel 33270, 30207, Tlx 292-368

SPARTA TRAVEL & TOURIST AGENCY
5, Ricou Arcade, near Cyprus Square, P.O. Box 122
Tel 24646, 20355, Tlx 292-143, Cbl Spart-Rhodes
Member of: IATA (code 27-2 2228)

TRANS-MARITIME Ltd., SHIPPING & TRANSPORTATIONS Co.,
1A, 25th Martiou Str. P.O. Box 247, Tel 25511, 21636, 26997.,
Tlx 292-228

TRAVELAIR HOLIDAYS S.A.
42, Akti Miaouli, Tel 29214, 29291, Tlx 292-260

TRAVELAND
71, Othonos & Amalias Str. P.O. Box 50
Tel 26291, 30527, 30533, Tlx 292-233
General Sales Agents for Iberia Airlines

TRAVELCO TOURS Ltd.
5, I. Dragoumi Str. Tel 28040, 28464, 30675, Tlx 292-283
General Sales Agents in Dodecanese for SAS.

TRITON HOLIDAYS
25, N. Plastira Str. P.O. Box 84, off. Cyprus Square
Tel 21778, 21690, 26414, 21691, 82203, Tlx 292-422

VISITELLAS TOURIST SERVICES Ltd.
9, Akti Kanari, P.O. Box 176, Tel 20705, 30102, 21822,
Tlx 292-296

ZANETOS TRAVEL
17, 25th Martiou Str. Tel 22470, Tlx 292-114
General Sales Agents for Austrian Airlines

interfurs

27-30, Ippocratous Sq. Rodos. Tel: 0241-29802

KEY TO MAP

═══════	ASPHALT—PAVED ROAD
═══════	NON—ASPHALT ROAD
════════	ROAD UNDER CONSTRUCTION
⸱ 8 ⸱	DISTANCES IN KILOMETRES
✈	AIRPORT
⚓	YACHT SUPPLY STATION
⛨	ARCHAEOLOGICAL SITE
⛨	BYZANTINE SITE
⌂	MEDIEVAL SITE
⛪	MONASTERY
⚕	SPA RESORT
⛱	BEACH
⛳	GOLF COURCE

«CHARTOGRAPHICA HELLENICA» DEMETRIUS G. TSOPELA

MONTE SMITH

KRITIKA

FILERIMOS-IALISSOS-AIRPORT

ARTOGRAPHICA HELLENICA» DEMETRIUS G. TSOPELAS ©

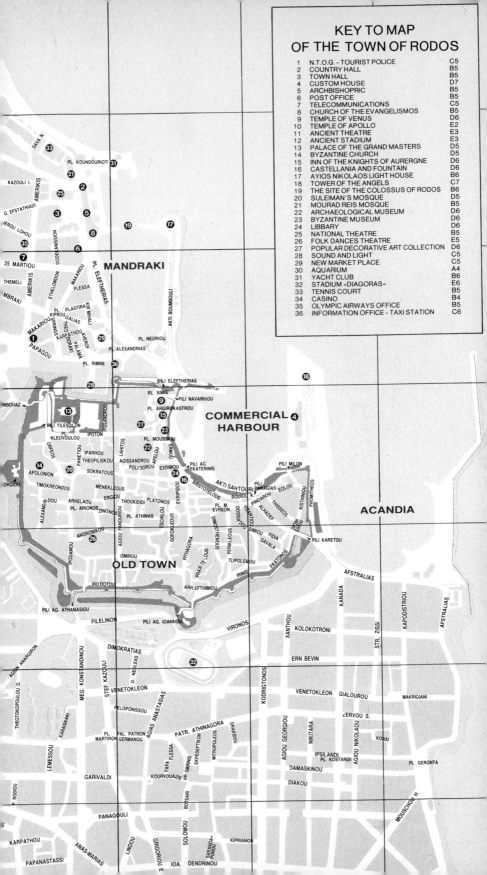

KEY TO MAP
OF THE TOWN OF RODOS

1	N.T.O.G. - TOURIST POLICE	C5
2	COUNTRY HALL	B5
3	TOWN HALL	B5
4	CUSTOM HOUSE	D7
5	ARCHBISHOPRIC	B5
6	POST OFFICE	B5
7	TELECOMMUNICATIONS	C5
8	CHURCH OF THE EVANGELISMOS	B5
9	TEMPLE OF VENUS	D6
10	TEMPLE OF APOLLO	E2
11	ANCIENT THEATRE	E3
12	ANCIENT STADIUM	E3
13	PALACE OF THE GRAND MASTERS	D5
14	BYZANTINE CHURCH	D5
15	INN OF THE KNIGHTS OF AURERGNE	D6
16	CASTELLANIA AND FOUNTAIN	D6
17	AYIOS NIKOLAOS LIGHT HOUSE	B6
18	TOWER OF THE ANGELS	C7
19	THE SITE OF THE COLOSSUS OF RODOS	B6
20	SULEIMAN'S MOSQUE	D5
21	MOURAD REIS MOSQUE	B5
22	ARCHAEOLOGICAL MUSEUM	D6
23	BYZANTINE MUSEUM	D6
24	LIBBARY	D6
25	NATIONAL THEATRE	B5
26	FOLK DANCES THEATRE	E5
27	POPULAR DECORATIVE ART COLLECTION	D6
28	SOUND AND LIGHT	C5
29	NEW MARKET PLACE	C5
30	AQUARIUM	A4
31	YACHT CLUB	B6
32	STADIUM «DIAGORAS»	E6
33	TENNIS COURT	B5
34	CASINO	B4
35	OLYMPIC AIRWAYS OFFICE	B5
36	INFORMATION OFFICE - TAXI STATION	C6

MANDRAKI

COMMERCIAL HARBOUR

ACANDIA

OLD TOWN

HOTEL INDEX

Hotel	Category	Town	Rodos Map
1. ACANDIA HOTEL	B΄	RODOS	B5
2. ACHILLION HOTEL	C΄	RODOS	A4
3. ADONIS HOTEL	C΄	RODOS	B5
4. AEGEON HOTEL	C΄	RODOS	C4
5. AEGLI HOTEL	C΄	RODOS	E7
6. AFRICA HOTEL	C΄	RODOS	C4
7. AFRODITI (VENUS) HOTEL	C΄	RODOS	B4
8. AGLAIA HOTEL	B΄	RODOS	C3
9. ALEXANDROS HOTEL	B΄	RODOS	
10. ALEXIA HOTEL	B΄	RODOS	B4
11. ALIA APARTMENTS	B΄	IXIA	
12. ALKYON HOTEL	D΄	RODOS	
13. ALS HOTEL	C΄	RODOS	B4
14. AMARYLLIS HOTEL	C΄	RODOS	B4
15. AMAZONA HOTEL	C΄	RODOS	
16. AMBASSADEUR HOTEL	C΄	RODOS	B4
17. AMPHITHEATER APARTMENTS	B΄	LINDOS	
18. AMPHITRION HOTEL	B΄	RODOS	C5
19. ANASTASIA HOTEL	D΄	NEOCHORION	
20. ANGELA HOTEL	B΄	RODOS	C4
21. ANTHOULA HOTEL	C΄	RODOS	
22. APOLLO BEACH HOTEL	A΄	FALIRAKI	
23. APOLLONIA HOTEL APARTMENTS	A΄	IXIA	
24. AQUARIUS APARTMENTS	B΄	RODOS	
25. ARCHANGELOS HOTEL	D΄	ARCHANGELOS	
26. ARIETTE HOTEL	D΄	RODOS	
27. ARION HOTEL	C΄	RODOS	C5
28. ASTORIA HOTEL	C΄	RODOS	C5
29. ASTRON HOTEL	C΄	RODOS	B5
30. ATHINA HOTEL	B΄	NEOCHORION	B4
31. ATHINEA PENSION	C΄	RODOS	
32. ATLANTIS HOTEL	C΄	RODOS	B4
33. ATLAS HOTEL	D΄	RODOS	B4
34. ATTALIA HOTEL (INN)	E΄	RODOS	
35. ATTIKI HOTEL (INN)	E΄	RODOS	
36. AVRA BEACH HOTEL	A΄	IXIA	
37. BELLA VISTA HOTEL	B΄	RODOS	A4
38. BEL AIR HOTEL	A΄	IXIA	
39. BELVEDERE HOTEL	A΄	RODOS	C3
40. BILLY'S APTS.	C΄	FALIRAKI	
41. BLUE BAY HOTEL AND APARTMENTS	A΄	IALYSSOS	
42. BLUE HORIZON HOTEL	A΄	TRIANDA	
43. BLUE SEA HOTEL	A΄	FALIRAKI	
44. BLUE SKY HOTEL	A΄	RODOS	C3
45. BOUCAINVILLEA HOTEL	C΄	FALIRAKI	
46. CABANA HOTEL	E΄	RODOS	A4
47. CACTUS HOTEL	B΄	RODOS	C5
48. CAIRO PALACE HOTEL	A΄	FALIRAKI	
49. CALYPSO HOTEL	A΄	RODOS	D5
50. CARACAS HOTEL	C΄	IXIA	
51. CARAVEL HOTEL APARTMENTS	A΄	RODOS	B4
52. CARINA HOTEL	C΄	RODOS	B4
53. CHEVALIER'S PALACE HOTEL	A΄	FALIRAKI	
54. COLOSSOS BEACH CLUB HOTEL	A΄	RODOS	
55. CONGO HOTEL	C΄	RODOS	B5
56. CONSTANTINOS HOTEL	B΄	RODOS	E4
57. CONTINENTAL HOTEL	B΄	RODOS	A4 & B4
58. CORALI HOTEL	B΄	RODOS	
59. COVA BEACH HOTEL	E΄	RODOS	
60. CRITI HOTEL	E΄	AFANDOU	
61. DESPINA PENSION	A΄	RODOS	C5
62. DESPO HOTEL	B΄	RODOS	B4
63. DIANA HOTEL	C΄	FALIRAKI	
64. DIMITRA HOTEL	C΄	RODOS	B5
65. DIETHNES HOTEL	C΄	IXIA	
66. DIONYSOS HOTEL	A΄	RODOS	
67. DORA PENSION	E΄	THEOLOGOS	
68. DORETA BEACH HOTEL	A΄	RODOS	B4
69. D'OR HOTEL	D΄	FALIRAKI	
70. EDELWEISS HOTEL	C΄	RENI KOSKINOU	
71. EDEN ROC HOTEL	A΄	AFANDOU	
72. EFKALYPTOS HOTEL	E΄	RODOS	
73. EFROSSINI HOTEL	D΄	PROFITIS ELIAS	
74. ELAFOS - ELAFINA HOTEL	A΄	TRIANDA	
75. ELECTRA PALACE HOTEL	A΄	RODOS	B5
76. EL GRECO HOTEL	C΄		

63

Hotel	Category	Town	Rodos Map
77. ELINA HOTEL	A˙	IXIA	
78. ELISABETH HOTEL APARTHMENTS	A˙	RODOS	
79. ELITE HOTEL	C˙	RODOS	
80. EMBONA HOTEL	C˙	RODOS	A4 & A5
81. ERODIA HOTEL APARTMENTS	B˙	RODOS	B4
82. ESAIAS HOTEL APARTMENTS	A˙	RODOS	
83. ESPERIA HOTEL	B˙	RODOS	B4
84. ESPERIDES HOTEL	A˙	FALIRAKI	
85. ESPEROS HOTEL	A˙	FALIRAKI	
86. EVA APARTMENTS	A˙	RODOS	B5
87. EVI HOTEL	C˙	FALIRAKI	
88. EUROPA HOTEL	B˙	RODOS	B4 & C4
89. FALIRAKI BEACH HOTEL	A˙	FALIRAKI	
90. FALIRON HOTEL	E˙	FALIRAKI	
91. FIESTA HOTEL	E˙	FALIRAKI	
92. FILERIMOS HOTEL APARTMENTS	A˙	RODOS	
93. FIVOS HOTEL	D˙	ARCHANGELOS	
94. FLORA HOTEL	C˙	RODOS	C4
95. FLORIDA HOTEL	C˙	RODOS	B5
96. FOTINI HOTEL	C˙	RODOS	
97. FOUR SEASONS HOTEL	C˙	RODOS	B4
98. FRANTZIDIS HOTEL APARTMENTS	C˙	RODOS	
99. GALATIA PENSION	C˙	RODOS	
100. GALAXIAS HOTEL	C˙	RODOS	
101. GEORGE HOTEL	B˙	RODOS	C3
102. GOLDEN BEACH HOTEL	A˙	IXIA	
103. GRAND HOTEL ASTIR PALACE	L	RODOS	B4
104. GREEN VIEW HOTEL	C˙	RODOS	
105. HELENA HOTEL	C˙	RODOS	B4
106. HELIOS HOTEL	A˙	RODOS	
107. HERMES HOTEL	C˙	RODOS	C5
108. IALYSSOS BAY HOTEL	A˙	IALYSSOS	
109. IALYSSOS HOTEL	E˙	RODOS	
110. IATRIDES APTS	C˙	FALIRAKI	
111. IBISCUS HOTEL	A˙	RODOS	A4& A5
112. IDEAL HOTEL APARTMENTS	C˙	FALIRAKI	
113. ILIOVASSILEMA HOTEL	C˙	THEOLOGOS	
114. IMPALA APARTMENTS	C˙	RODOS	
115. IMPERIAL HOTEL	A˙	RODOS	B5
116. INTEUROPA APTS	B˙	RODOS	
117. IRENE HOTEL	C˙	RODOS	C5
118. IRIS HOTEL	D˙	RODOS	B4
119. ISABELLA HOTEL	C˙	RODOS	C4
120. JOHANNES HOTEL	E˙	AFANDOU	
121. JOLLY GUEST HOUSE	B˙	RODOS	
122. KAMIROS HOTEL	A˙	RODOS	C5
123. KARMEN APTS	C˙	RODOS	
124. KASTRO HOTEL	E˙	RODOS	
125. KYPRIOTIS HOTEL	C˙	RODOS	
126. LA LUNA HOTEL	E˙	RODOS	
127. LEFKA HOTEL	B˙	RODOS	
128. LIA PENSION	C˙	RODOS	
129. LIDO HOTEL	C˙	FALIRAKI	
130. LINDOS BAY HOTEL	A˙	LINDOS	
131. LISA GUEST HOUSE	C˙	IALYSSOS	
132. LITO HOTEL	B˙	IXIA	
133. LOMENIZ HOTEL	B˙	RODOS	
134. LYDIA HOTEL	C˙	RODOS	C5
135. MAJESTIC HOTEL	C˙	RODOS	C4
136. MANDRAKI HOTEL	C˙	RODOS	
137. MANIAS APTS	C	FALIRAKI	
138. MANOUSOS HOTEL	B	RODOS	B4
139. MARGET HOTEL	E˙	RODOS	
140. MARIE HOTEL	C˙	RODOS	B5
141. MARIETTE HOTEL APARTMENTS	C˙	RODOS	
142. MARINA HOTEL	E˙	RODOS	
143. MARNIN HOTEL	E˙	RODOS	
144. MASSARI PENSION	C˙	RODOS	
145. MATSIS HOTEL	E˙	RODOS	
146. MEDITERRANEAN HOTEL	A˙	RODOS	A5
147. METROPOLITAN CAPSIS HOTEL	A˙	IXIA	
148. MIMOZA HOTEL	C˙	RODOS	B5
149. MINOS HOTEL	C˙	RODOS	C5
150. MIRAMARE BEACH	L	IXIA	
151. MONTE SMITH HOTEL APARTMENTS	A˙	RODOPOULA	
152. MOSCHOS HOTEL	C˙	RODOS	C5
153. MOURATIS HOTEL	E˙	KALATHOS	
154. MOUSSES HOTEL BUNGALOWS	B˙	FALIRAKI	
155. NAFSIKA HOTEL	C˙	RODOS	
156. NEST (FOLIA) HOTEL	E˙	RODOS	
157. NEW VILAGGE INN HOTEL	E˙	RODOS	

Hotel	Category	Town	Rodos Map
158. NEW YORK HOTEL	C	RODOS	B4
159. NOUFARA HOTEL	C	RODOS	C5
160. OASSIS HOLIDAYS HOTEL BUNGALOWS	A	AFANDOU	
161. OASSIS HOTEL	B	RODOS	
162. OCEANIS HOTEL	A	IXIA	
163. ODYSIA HOTEL	E	FALIRAKI	
164. OLYMPIC HOTEL	B	RODOS	A4
165. OLYMPIC PALACE HOTEL	L	IXIA	
166. ORION APTS	C	RODOS	
167. PAHOS HOTEL APARTMENTS	B	IALYSSOS	
168. PALLADION HOTEL	C	RODOS	C4
169. PANTHEON HOTEL	D	RODOS	C5
170. PARADISE HOTEL	A	RENI KOSKINOU	
171. PARIS HOTEL	D	RODOS	
172. PARK HOTEL	A	RODOS	D4
173. PARTHENON HOTEL	C	RODOS	C4
174. PAVLIDIS HOTEL	C	RODOS	C4
175. PEARL HOTEL	C	RODOS	C4
176. PEGASOS HOTEL	A	FALIRAKI	
177. PETALOUDA HOTEL	C	RODOS	C4
178. PHAEDRA HOTEL	C	RODOS	C3
179. PHAEDRA HOTEL	D	LARDOS	
180. PHOENIX (PALM) HOTEL	B	RODOS	A4 & A5
181. PLATANOS HOTEL	E	FALIRAKI	
182. PLAZA HOTEL	B	RODOS	B5
183. POSEIDON HOTEL	B	RODOS	
184. POSSIDONIA HOTEL	A	IXIA	
185. PSAROPOULA HOTEL	E	RODOS	
186. PYLONA HOTEL	E	PYLONA	
187. REGINA HOTEL	A	RODOS	C5
188. REX HOTEL	D	RODOS	C4
189. RHEA HOTEL	E	FALIRAKI	
190. RHODIAKON HOTEL	D	RODOS	C3
191. RHODIAN VILLAGE HOLIDAYS HOTEL	E	RODOS	
192. RIVIERA HOTEL	A	RODOS	A4 & B4
193. RODOS BAY HOTEL	A	IXIA	
194. RODOS BEACH HOTEL	A	FALIRAKI	
195. RODOS PALACE HOTEL	L	IXIA	
196. RODINI HOTEL	D	RODOS	
197. ROMA HOTEL	C	IXIA	
198. ROYAL HOTEL	C	RODOS	C5
199. SAINT AMON HOTEL	E	FALIRAKI	
200. SAINT ANTONIO HOTEL	C	RODOS	B4
201. SANDY COAST HOTEL APARTMENTS	B	RODOS	G6
202. SANTA MARIA HOTEL	C	RODOS	
203. SARONIS HOTEL	C	RODOS	B4
204. SAVOY HOTEL	C	RODOS	C5
205. SEMIRAMIS HOTEL	C	RODOS	C3 & C4
206. SIRAVAST HOTEL	A	RODOS	A4
207. SIRENE HOTEL	A	KRITIKA	
208. SOLEIL HOTEL	C	RODOS	D5
209. SOLEMAR HOTEL	B	IXIA	
210. SOPHIA HOTEL	C	FALIRAKI	
211. SPARTALIS HOTEL	B	RODOS	C5
212. STAR HOTEL	D	RODOS	
213. STELLA GUEST HOUSE	B	RODOS	
214. STEPS OF LINDOS HOTEL	A	RODOS	
215. STEVE HOTEL	E	RODOS	
216. SUN BEACH HOTEL	A	IALYSSOS	
217. SUN PALACE HOTEL	A	FALIRAKI	
218. SUNRISE FURNISHED APARTMENTS	B	RODOS	B4
219. SUN WING HOTEL	A	RODOS	
220. SYDNEY HOTEL	E	RODOS	
221. SYLVIA HOTEL	C	RODOS	E7
222. SYMI HOTEL (INN)	E	RODOS	
223. TEHERANI HOTEL	E	RODOS	
224. THERMAE HOTEL	B	RODOS	C4 & C5
225. THOLOS HOTEL	C	THEOLOGOS	
226. TILOS HOTEL	C	RODOS	C5
227. VASSILIA HOTEL	C	RODOS	B4
228. VELLOIS HOTEL	C	IXIA	
229. VERINO APARTHOTEL	A	RODOS	
230. VICTORIA HOTEL	C	RODOS	C5
231. VILLA HELENA (APARTMENTS)	C	PARADISSI	
232. VILLA RHODOS	C	NEOCHORION	
233. VIOLETTA HOTEL	B	FALIRAKI	
234. WING APARTMENTS	B	IXIA	
235. XANTHI HOTEL	D	RODOS	C4
236. XENIA GOLF	B	AFANDOU	
237. ZEPHYROS HOTEL	D	RODOS	
238. ZEUS HOTEL	C	RODOS	

69

Key to symbols and abbreviations

rm   rooms

bung   bungalows

apt   apartments

Central heating

Air-conditioning

Rooms with telephone

Rooms with music

Rooms with T.V.

Rooms with private shower and toilet

Rooms with private bath and toilet

Rooms with air-conditioning

Restaurant

Self-service

Taverna

Bar

Cafeteria

Daily room-service

24 hour room-service

Cleaner's

Hairdresser's

Kindergarten

Pets allowed overnight

Discotheque

Swimming-pool

"Private" beach

Beach with water sports facilities

Tennis Court

Courts for other sports

Open Parking

Garage

(C.C.)   Credit Cards

Organized excursions/tours

REPORT FORM

Please help us bring this publication up-to-date by commenting on the hotels you have stayed in.

Thank you!

To **Tourist Publications**
15, Spyrou Trikoupi Str.
106 83 Athens GREECE

Name of Hotel ....

Address ....

Category ....

Did you find:	Very Good	Satisfactory	Below Expectation
Accommodation	☐	☐	☐
Service	☐	☐	☐
Meals	☐	☐	☐

Do you agree with the contents of the list of hotels in this Guide? YES ☐ NO ☐

If you disagree have you any remarks to make?

....
....
....
....

Name: ....

Address: ....

....

Date: ....

Signature:

Notes: